G.P.S.:
Grounded in Gratitude
Plotting New Coordinates
Set to Soar

Praise for

G.P.S. to Joy

G.P.S. to Joy *lives up to its title and so much more. If you are going through a tough period in your life or a major transition and feel you are stuck, then this book is for you. We all can go through huge trauma in our lives and we can heal and grow from it. This book provides practical advice with exercises that will empower and transform your life, no matter what you have been through. Maryl has her own story of adversity and has come out on the other side with joy, and so she speaks with experience and amazing wisdom.*

~ Kim Quick
Premier Love Coach,
Forever Love Formula

About G.P.S. to Joy, *all I can say is, WOW! Bottom line: Maryl's words have helped me unlock my joy! I have gone from unclear to clarity by using the process. I have an amazing experience of true joy in my relationship and a new level of performance in my business with confidence and peace of mind. This book helped me move forward quickly.*

Maryl has a gentle and engaging writing style that very quickly replaces fog and fear with peace and deep clarity. Her mentoring in the book has moved me into NEW actions that have up-leveled my love life and my business success.

With G.P.S. to Joy, *I'm clear on what brings me joy and what doesn't, and I now have an extraordinary love and powerful results in my business that definitely came from me getting clarity for myself using her process and letting go of ways of approaching love and business that weren't working.*

Her mastery as a coach entails digging directly to the underbelly of the obstacles and aiding in releasing them, so you powerfully move forward to have what you want.

~ Carmen Torres
CEO & Chief Specialist
My HR Specialist
Www.myhrspecialist.com

G.P.S. to Joy is exactly the book I needed at the right time! The guidance it provides is fast and simple to use. It has made my experience as a new empty nester so much easier to navigate. I've used the Joy Activation Process on different challenges and it really works! If you are an empty nester or have just gone through a really hard life event, this book is a great remedy to moving through to the other side.

~ Curtis W. Lewis
A/P U.S. History Teacher
Poway High School, Poway, CA

Maryl has been a source of inspiration for me in many ways. First, her ability to ask questions that prompt me to look at areas that I had not thought of and get surprising new insights, answers, and actions. She also has been a great teacher, and I've learned to change my perceptions and develop new ideas and ways to handle triggers and loops from the past. Lastly, her vast business experience has helped guide me through some of the most difficult business decisions in my career.

I highly recommend her.

~ Hazel Ortega
Ortega Counseling Center
Author, From Bounced Checks to Private Jets: The Mastery of Miracles

This is a captivating and real world tool that anyone can use to get their life back on track! It is even suitable to use as a tool to ensure good practices in your life and support you mind, body and soul. This is a must read!!!!!

I highly recommend her.

~ Marie McNeal
Intuitive Life Coach

G.P.S. to Joy

Navigate Life's Turbulence & Toughest Transitions to Find Your New Direction

By Maryl Petreccia, The #JOYEXPERT and Creator of the Joy Activation Process™

G.P.S. to Joy
Navigate Life's Turbulence & Toughest Transitions to Find Your New Direction

Published by Joyful Life Publishing
360 East 1st Street #954
Tustin, CA 92780

A Joyful Life Series

Cover design by Jim Saurbaugh, JS Graphic Design

Dedicated ~

To my late husband, David, dream launcher extraordinaire. To my parents, Bobbi and Marvin, who grounded me. To my sister, who brought me back to life. To my daughter, Helena, who keeps me growing. And to all you I love, whether I've met you or not. Thank you all for fueling my joy tank and supporting the writing of this book.

Table of Contents

Foreword

I first met Maryl Petreccia through personal transformation programs at Landmark Worldwide. When I met her, she was feverishly trying to get her head above water. Anyone who has been there knows that losing important people in your life can really take you out of the game. Maryl lost her father, mother, and husband in a four-year span. She became an empty nester: her stepchildren had left home and her daughter moved to college out-of-state. She moved residences and rebuilt where she was living, from the ground up.

She had lost the joy in her life, and she knew it. But she didn't fold in on herself and give up. Instead, she began to unfold herself into a thousand pieces on the floor. She picked them up and began to put herself back together.

Maryl did everything from personal growth and development to therapy to getting financial consulting. I saw her in several transformational programs over a period of ten years. When I first met her, she was raw. Then I watched as she recreated herself—choice by choice, step by step, and year by year. She created a new trajectory for her life. There was a point at which she made a choice, and she refused to be sad any more. The last time I saw her, I told her, "I don't know what you have been doing, but I want some of that!"

I saw her transformation in her physical appearance and the things she said. When I first met her, I noticed she was sad much of the time, yet I knew she was amazing underneath. Then, it became clear to me that she had made a choice to have joy back in her life. She got young, energetic, alive, and light. She appeared to flow through life—even her hair got bouncy! She began to take on the idea that her words create her world. Every conversation became something like, "Oh, my gosh! Guess what I'm up to!" She got that she could have a great life as a choice. She took on a new direction for herself in every aspect of her life—in where she lived, how she spent her time, in her love life, and for her business.

Maryl has been an innovator in business from the age of 23 when she was recognized as having the best business idea and launch by the Los Angeles Chapter of Women in Business. She invented an eco-friendly, biodegradable product for the beauty business and became very successful—even landing Estée Lauder as a client—in an industry that is for women but chiefly run by men. And she did it 35 years ago when the path was even harder for women.

She was a visionary then, and she is a visionary today. She created the Joy Activation Process for people, particularly women, in the midst of massive transitions to get grounded, find their new bearings and navigate their joy. She has become an expert in joy and provides an easy-to-follow guide for people who feel adrift in some way to reinvent their lives from what truly brings them joy.

Jo Blackwell-Preston
CEO and President of Dop Dop Salon, Soho, New York City and
L'Oréal Professionelle International Artist

Preface

My name is Maryl Petreccia, and I am the Joy Expert. You could be thinking, "That's a pretty big claim." What gives me the right to make it? Well, I lost my mother, my father, and my husband inside a four-year period. In addition, my daughter left for out-of-state college, my adult step-kids were out of the house living on their own, and I sold the family home to move closer to the hospital as my husband's terminal cancer progressed quickly. My businesses suffered when I neglected them, and my role shifted completely to caregiver. You could say that everything that had given me my life purpose and a future were gone. I'd lost my true north and everything I'd used to navigate my life.

How does that lead to joy for me or any of us?

We've all been there, finding ourselves overcome by life's travails and drowning under the weight of them, barely able to stay afloat – lost. Loss, sadness, and tragedy come with being human, as does going to emotionally painful places when we face our failings.

In the challenge of personal tragedy, I found triumph over fear, and I weathered life's roughest storms. I discovered the power and capacity for perseverance, and that gave me the will to continue during these upheavals. It's what tragedy often does for us. It also broke my heart wide open and uprooted me something awful. The life I had known, with all of the roles and responsibilities that had grounded me, had vanished far too quickly.

I rose again and again, pulling myself up from one loss after the next. Along the way, I found the strength and wisdom to navigate toward the gold inside each transition.

The gold I found? JOY. As I struggled and grieved and grew, I dug deeper and I found ME—beautiful, raw, and real.

I confronted my circumstances and came up against the limits of my constraints. I looked within and watched as a clear path to joy systematically came into view. That's when I became the Joy Expert. That's when I understood that anyone could navigate back to joy and that **we all** are our very own joy expert.

When you were younger, did it ever occur to you in your wildest dreams that you would pick up and start reading a book titled, *G.P.S. to Joy*, a book about reinventing your life and navigating your joy? I certainly didn't. There wasn't even a remote possibility that I would someday find myself in need of navigating my JOY—whatever that meant!

Then my life happened, and happened again. Life's complexities continued to take me beyond my edge of comfort. Some days, they siphoned my energy, and I became more exhausted with each transition. The major impact was that my experience of happiness was plummeting. I was losing IT. I was losing my joy. I felt lost, even adrift.

Being pushed to our edges and losing joy seems unavoidable because life is unpredictable. Events happen that we simply cannot reconcile or control. Those trials and transitions can shake us to our core. That happened to me repeatedly.

Pick a life transition, just about any transition. Make it life-altering, uprooting, unraveling, and *really hard*—in fact, let's throw in heart-wrenching, just for good measure — and I've lived through it, like so many of us.

By virtue of losing everything I knew, I discovered what truly fills me with joy and what elevates me. I discovered deeper aspects of myself that I really like!

I connected to my capacity for resilience. I built the muscle to dream again and uncovered what brings me true joy. I unfolded my life's work, all from a promise that I made to my late husband a few days before he died.

It also led me to write this book — the one I believe can truly help you reinvent your life and navigate your joy again.

Preface

Part 1: Grounded... with Gratitude

You've been grounded. I know that because you are reading this book. You might be feeling lost. You can't begin to think about navigating anything right now because you don't even know which way to turn. You might even feel like you are drowning and not sure which direction has more oxygen.

The sun has set on your personal horizon... perhaps that was caused by death, divorce, empty-nest syndrome, retirement, disconnection in your family... or any combination of those events or others. Regardless, the stars by which you'd navigated your life and your joy to this point have disappeared from your sky. You struggle to imagine tomorrow with any sense of hope, let alone joy, because you simply feel lost.

I get it. As I've shared, I was there.

The rudder of your life that was defined by your roles to this point is broken. Maybe you're a widow now rather than a wife. Or you've become an ex-spouse. Your role as parent has changed dramatically as your children have moved out and moved on to their adult lives. Yes, you're still the parent, but that role is far different than it was, and you need to adjust. Maybe a death in the family has upended your role as caregiver. Perhaps you're no longer headed for the office each day, wearing your job title as another role in your life that gave you direction.

Yup. You're grounded.

There's another meaning in "grounded" that we must also consider and think about, and it finds its place in those things that keep us down... stuck... lacking joy. For example, if you are continuing to remain in a toxic relationship (regardless of whether it's with a spouse, family member, or friend), you are grounding yourself... and you've chosen to remain there because the idea of cutting that anchor is too frightening. If you remain in an unfulfilling career or role of any type, you are grounding yourself. If you can see yourself in these situations or similar ones, you are navigating away from joy, and it's time to free yourself.

No matter how scary it may seem, you cannot navigate toward joy until you release yourself from the negative anchors in your life that keep you grounded in a very negative way.

But there's a ray of light on the horizon – charting a brand new course starts with being lost. You can get "unlost," and that's what I'll help you do. I want you to ground yourself in gratitude about the changes that have occurred in your life bringing you to this point.

Wait. Did I just suggest that you should be grateful for all that has happened? Yes. Be grounded in gratitude because charting your new course and navigating toward joy all starts with being lost and feeling adrift. Only when you've lost sight of the stars in your life by which you've navigated can you move on to find your new true north.

Chapter One:

Adrift and Rudderless

"All the art of living lies in the fine mingling of letting go and holding on." ~ Havelock Ellis

Death. Grief. Illness. Heart-wrenching transitions.

Like so many people, I had a normal reaction to three consecutive deaths in my family. I was emotionally raw, very much on edge, and crestfallen in ways that had me not able to recognize myself. Between 2010 and 2014, my heart was shattered by the loss of my father, then my mother, and then my husband, David. We were all close, so losing them really unsettled me. In short, almost all that had given me my purpose and future was gone. I was adrift and definitely rudderless.

You could say I lost it all—my roles, the vision for my life, a future filled with all that my husband and I had dreamed about. My life was upended, my heart ached and the uncertainty of it gave me no time to come up for air. I'd lost all my bearings and was completely stalled.

The roadmap and charts that had taken years to plan and refine were gone. I had lost direction and a clear vision for where I belonged and where I needed to be. Beyond grieving, I was majorly perimenopausal, a reluctant empty nester, and without a nuclear family or home. We had sold our house, so I could move closer to the hospital where my husband was a patient.

My daily diet was grief and brain fog. If it hadn't been for friends, I literally would not have eaten. My naiveté around control put me into a tailspin. I had always coped by controlling, and when I couldn't control the circumstances, I got completely off-kilter. Admitting how much this made me suffer was not easy. I decided to make a shift.

I started to let go where I was over-attached, and I gained discernment around what I actually *could* control. It boiled down to this: where I belonged and what I was meant to do would possibly be beyond my control. What I could control was my point of view or how I saw and interpreted anything. I couldn't choose when people died and when I had to downsize or move on. I couldn't stop life from completely altering, but I could choose the filter I used to make sense of major life loss and transitions. I could decide to re-start my stalled engine and begin to move forward on a new course that would invariably put me in a new direction.

Critical transitions call for critical triage. In medicine, triage is the assignment of degrees of urgency to determine the order in which patients should be treated. Those missing a limb get treated first while those with a lesser laceration wait. Triage occurs when there are a large number of patients, all of whom need medical attention. Choosing who to treat first can seem impossible. In the midst of my personal challenges, I was not sure which parts of my life needed immediate attention and which could wait. It was hard to see.

In the last days of my husband's life, I could see deep sadness in his eyes. He was worried about how I'd carry on without him. In that moment, I made a vow to him: I promised him that I would be okay and would live the most extraordinary life I could. I admitted that I didn't know how to do that, but I told him that I would honor the gift of love that he had given me every day going forward.

After he died, I shifted my attention to my own self-care. I turned my attention inward. My first goal? Don't die of a broken heart. My second goal? Live moment by moment and unfold myself—thought by thought, choice by choice, action by action, dream by dream.

I had a pivotal choice to make: succumb to sadness or reinvent my life. For the latter, I would need to revamp my mindset and find a new kind of courage.

I had been a dancer for more than ten years. In my mind's eye, I imagined myself in the midst of a volatile dance whose choreography would be executed with beauty and grace as I transformed, but not at first! There was no question I was off balance and floundering,

> *The choice: succumb to sadness or reinvent and find joy.*

but I knew I had to keep moving. With each new movement, my form improved, and my dancing flowed better. However, at the height of each loss, I did my best to muster the will to press on because joy was still outside my reach.

Pain flattened me. Still, I would fall back on that promise I made to David by asking one question again and again: What brings me joy? It could be a cup of tea on the balcony. It might be simply putting on my favorite pair of shoes. Each choice I made when I asked that question made room for small sparks of happiness through the cracks of sorrow – one new little star by which I could navigate starting to shine. Just the process of asking and answering

13

made the next action easy and obvious. This was the start of the Joy Activation Process. From that beginning, a method and some simple practices emerged. These practices guided me and gave me the ability to reinvent every detail of my life. They helped me plot my course toward joy.

I came alive by feeling my emotions in real time. I got physically strong again in the gym. I moved into a new town. I experienced more grace through my dancing by expressing gratitude, accepting the generosity of others, and being generous with myself and others. I wrote poetry and meditated; I prayed and released the attachments and attitudes that no longer served me – some of the anchors that were negatively grounding me.

I slowly built my confidence again by releasing excess baggage like worry and fear of the unknown and trusting the process of change. I played again by getting more resilient. My friendships became more sacred, and I honored myself in whole new ways.

With time, my passion for life came back. I experienced my sensuality and beauty again. I laughed more and lightened up. I was transforming. I was finding and navigating my joy.

Accepting the Unacceptable

One of the biggest accomplishments was realizing the command I had over my point of view. That alone gave me strength and balance. I also noticed, both for myself and others, how often we feel stuck and are stopped by our fears, silently (or not so silently) suffering by tolerating the intolerable. I distinguished how we are dimmed to our own light, beauty, and power. I saw how many of us don't see

14

our unique and extraordinary capacities and our own magnificence. I wondered why.

Here's what became so obvious. Many of us have this invasive inner critic that lives like a virus in our heads. It's this incessant inner chatter that can really throw us off! The other big culprit is our tendency to second guess. That puts such a damper on us. Both that voice and the second guessing are major life buzz-killers! And what does the inner critic generally say? "Not good enough; you could do better. What if that doesn't work out? Better not... might get it wrong." Oh, the havoc it wreaks!

Even more startling was noticing the diminished self-regard we have to which we are so unconscious! Sometimes when I people watch, I see the ways we carry ourselves and how we make ourselves physically smaller. It honestly breaks my heart when I hear people suppressing themselves with self-afflicted criticism, about their bodies, about their age, about their "screw ups." I became more sensitive to noticing how often we operate from our compulsion to do what's expected, no matter the cost to ourselves. I realized how we hold back on

> *Quiet your inner critic and stop second guessing your decisions.*

even having our truest dreams and hold joy captive, feeling imprisoned by expectations we think we need to meet because we believe, on some level, our very survival depends on it.

It can be so pervasive that I can sense when someone lives with deep-seated resignation. It's as if we already have what we deserve and we need to accept the circumstances as they are. All the while, we and everyone around us pay the price for our self-suppression—we forget how our own joys and dreams are crucial to nourish our lives and families.

This "wrangling" eventually reaches an understandable breaking point, and we get fed up and say, "Enough!" Or we lose everything, or even more likely, lose something so dear that we feel lost without it. Some pivotal event stirs us at a level that goes deeper than our self-deprecation.

Let me share my story.

Why Me?

I wrote this book for the person who is ready to move forward, to go deeper in their love for themselves and others and chooses to let love be the driver of their life choices. It is also for those who are fed up with habitual suffering and are no longer willing to be unraveled and stalled by life's circumstances. If you are reading this, I suspect that is very likely you. So, who am I and how am I qualified to have this very personal conversation with you?

I am you... a person who has learned how to be guided by love but who spent years being shaken up by so much that was *not* love in her daily reality. I am a person who has given too much of myself and had to up-level my self-care. Like you, I'm figuring life out as I go. I wrestle with the stickiness of perfection, getting it all right, and now I can more easily embrace my quirks and unique edges. I am well-intentioned and have often put others' needs before my own. This has left me suffering from time to time. I'm happy to report that as my own joy navigator, I am semi-retired from that sport!

I also finally made a truce with my inner critic. I can't put a full muzzle on it. But I do listen for a short time, look for the message, then after some internal negotiation, say, "Thank you," and breathe deeply until it loosens its grip. I realized that giving too much power and validity to this chatter leaves me feeling off balance, impacts my creativity, disrupts my love connections. If I let it, it can interfere with being present and awake to joy. That chatter keeps me on the defensive and puts my focus on getting things "right" and avoiding danger at all cost. Sound familiar? I'll bet it does!

For my personal history, I am a California native, a baby boomer, born in the early '60s into an immigrant family culture and mentality. It included a hyper-driven work ethic, a father who was both mom and dad, and a mother who was driven and chronically frustrated. My siblings and I were that decade's version of latchkey kids. I became a diplomat very early on as I navigated our family dynamic. It was impacted by my mom's melancholy and anxiety, family challenges, and my father's helplessness in dealing with it. Early on, I became accustomed to running for cover and striving for perfection to gain love and avoid rage. I was the standard first-born with all the accompanying responsibilities and attributes. I became "good" and looked outward for signals on how to manage my hidden insides. I learned very quickly how to steep myself in the armor of shame to avoid the danger of being exposed to even more pain.

In my scramble to survive challenging family dynamics, I squelched my self-expression and took refuge in organizing my world so I could have some version of a reliable structure. I developed an independent and capable exterior, yet I felt alone and unprotected during my earliest childhood transitions. Childhood was strained especially at the height of my parent's marital problems. My siblings and I were sent out-of-state to school. It was the age at which I felt entirely embarrassed by my changing body, my curly and uncontainable hair, and my relentlessly questioning brain!

After college in my early 20s, I rebelled by having love affairs. I fell for charming narcissists, some angry and both physically and emotionally unsafe. I received degrees from a prestigious college in economics and Spanish. Then I became an entrepreneur at age 21. Frankly, I did it because I lacked the confidence that I would ever figure out my true passion and didn't believe I was a good hire. So, what did I do? I joined the Los Angeles Chapter of Women in Business (WIB) and went on to receive the Women in Business Award for best business idea and launch at the age of 23. I became a solopreneur from that day forward. Women in Business was a national networking organization launched by leading women entrepreneurs to mentor, bring community to, and provide fundamental support and seed funding for women who were budding entrepreneurs. Just my bailiwick!

My education and entrepreneurial success sound great... on the surface. Yet, fundamentally, I was plagued with self-doubt, fearing that I would fail miserably. At my core, I felt helpless and overwhelmed in spite of being smart.

I had a very Jekyll and Hyde life: finding torment and struggle in love and seeking approval and credibility in business.

I married a man who was just like my mother (who doesn't?). The marriage was "challenging," the opposite of what every young woman dreams of. My ex-husband and mother even shared the same birthday for g-d sakes! Toward the end of my pregnancy with my daughter, toxemia forced a premature delivery that almost killed us both. I was too weak to nurse and she was too weak to feed. The thought of losing her almost did me in! But we survived.

When my daughter reached her sixth month, I left with her in my left arm and a diaper bag in my right, hiding his guns before the divorce papers arrived. With this marriage, I had put myself and my daughter in harm's way. My view of myself? Nothing great, to be completely straight.

I felt like a pathetic victim who should have known better. Some of my choices reflected that internal belief. My points of view about myself and my life had me in a chronic state of struggle, turmoil, and suffering. Why should I be surprised at that? It's what I knew well. I had grown up on a very robust diet of "it has to be hard" and "you must struggle to survive."

In navigating all of these transitions, I chose to confront these deeply held beliefs and emotions more and more openly and learned that they were mindsets and points of view at their core. Then something new emerged. Slowly, I began to see myself as beautiful, strong, and kind. I saw I was committed and loving. I set better boundaries and was done with mistreatment—beginning with the way I treated myself. I walked head-on through the fires of insecurity, fear, loneliness, and unworthiness.

I loved motherhood. Its key challenge came from a dysfunctional divorce that forced me to go through a heartbreaking custody arrangement in which my ex-husband gave my daughter a regular dose of toxic talk about me. This tested me, as well as my commitment to motherhood at a level I never could have imagined. I transitioned into receiving full custody from the court when she was 13 and then had the psychological fallout of that to manage through.

In the meantime, along came David, my late husband and partner since my daughter was 5-years-old. It was not a first marriage for either of us. I found love with him. In many ways, he was the man I had dreamed of. We had a

sweet love affair until he died in 2014. Our relationship was marred by our own respective histories, yet we expanded as much as our internal dealings would allow. We both wore protective armor to avoid emotional pain and to hide our deepest vulnerabilities. That being said, we knew it and were aware of our tendencies toward self-protection. We took on these "protective edges" together and grew ourselves into experiencing a profound love. My marriage, coupled with the transition of becoming a young widow, gave me a platform to reinvent from nothing and an opportunity to launch into who I am today. This is why I've grounded myself in gratitude for what I've endured – it has allowed me to truly find joy.

Your own story may be similar—we've all been there in small or large ways. We've been overcome by tough times and found ourselves adrift and rudderless. Oh man, is this a painful place to be!

When I looked under the lid of what challenged me, I became more vulnerable and found myself moving in the direction of joy. I discovered my potency. I grew and reinvented myself on the other side of the transitions. The roles that were the stars by which I navigated vanished with each transition or loss. That tested me. I overcame these losses and used them to uncover the treasures that were hidden inside. The sweetest treasure I found? Joy in being my true self. Inside the turbulence, I found *me*. Beautiful, raw, real, with my heart cracked wide open. And then—joy!

I remain a successful entrepreneur and dream launcher whose passion is traveling with you and your transitions as you navigate your own joy. I continue to discover the many sources of joy as my own #joyexpert, using pivotal transitions to reinvent every day. I love guiding people to discover the new stars to navigate by, to find their new bearings and course correct as they craft joy-filled lives.

This work stirs my soul! It's sacred. It's elevating. It's a joy! I look forward to traveling with you as you recalibrate your G.P.S. to joy. Let's get busy plotting your new coordinates!

Adrift and Rudderless

Chapter Two:

You Can't Avoid Turbulence

"Call them transitions. Call them disruptions. Call them heart-wrenching. Whatever we call them, they can take us off course in a big way." ~ *Maryl Petreccia*

So what does it mean to become your own joy navigator? Basically, navigating your joy is marrying your intention with your choices then taking new actions. It's a form of alignment that frees you up to move forward. As you integrate those components, you become the designer of your life, one choice and one challenge at time.

It is an understanding that your choices and actions, when interconnected with conscious intention, put you fully in charge of your life. In that place, you put yourself in alignment, find peace and experience deep joy.

Call them concerns. Call them transitions. Call them disruptions. Call them heart-wrenchers. Whatever we call them, they take us off course, often in a big way. But that's okay because charting a new course starts with being or getting lost. Although the sun may have set on your former horizon, the sun will always rise again. The tough challenges can make you reluctant to reposition, but I assure you, joy exists in realms that we cannot yet see. There are new stars to shine and new lands to discover.

So are you ready for joy? Are you willing to be a joy "adventurer" and even be your own joy expert? To qualify, you need to be willing to not know how to find it and to step forward into it anyway. Because that is what it will take. The path only materializes after you begin to take the steps. Joy uses our willingness, our desires, our vows, our transitions, our pains, our hesitations and resistances, and everything else in us to actualize our futures with new actions that are chosen to invite joy so a new "normal" can emerge.

The poet in me penned these words: *"I walked through the burning sands of my losses, with the sun scorching off the armor of my constraints, my defenses, and my fears that had cut me off from living full throttle. From the ashes, a woman of joy was reborn."*

In facing the requisite turmoil of these transitions, the Joy Activation Process unfolded. I discovered some of the most profound gifts of my life! I lightened up! I upgraded my mindset, took new actions, and found joy. I dropped my pretenses, became more vulnerable, and experienced abundance again—with family, friends, with vibrant moments, with finances, and more. My senses came alive! I could see more clearly, listen more deeply, bring more heartfelt compassion, have raw and honest conversations, feel more profoundly, let go of judgments more quickly, connect more lovingly with people, and play a lot more. I found joy again through gratitude and playfulness. I took my finances to a whole new level and experienced inner peace, self-trust, compassion, courage, and the capacity to go on, no longer needing to know what precisely came next.

I reinvented several aspects of my life and activated more *joy* as a result. These transitions gave me a new ME, beautiful and distinct, kind and wise.

This Book Is for You If:

- You're tired of living according to arbitrary standards of "shoulds" that no longer ring true for you and you're ready to be done with being hard on yourself.
- You have been tolerating the intolerable for too long, and this is no longer how you want to spend one more minute of your precious life!
- A part of you has given up. You've surrendered into a state of ambivalence (and are rudderless) because you've tried everything you know to move forward... and nothing is working.
- You feel conflicted in your priorities and you don't know how to be true to yourself and everything else you are committed to!
- You feel disconnected from who you really are and who and what you love, and you don't know how to rekindle your passion.
- You feel stalled and adrift in your goals for reasons that seem more real to you than a life you can envision and unfold.
- Until now, you have set your life aside and put others first. You know it's time to shift that. It's time to put your truest dreams into action.
- You want to feel fulfilled and happy and want to open your heart and mind to feel like you again!
- You are ready to take actions that elevate you.
- You want deeper relationships steeped in trust, honesty, compassion, and vulnerability.
- You're ready to trust the transitions and losses as life events that will launch a reinvented life.

- You have the courage to boldly step forward without needing to know what lies ahead.

To navigate your joy, you will use your vision and dreams to reinvent whatever you face and discover new horizons. Transitions give you the turbulence you need to right yourself and reset your G.P.S. to:

Ground yourself in Gratitude

Plot your new coordinates

Set yourself up to Soar

As you right yourself, you will be more of you and live from what you value most.

The Six Benefits and Promises of this Book

1. The Joy Activation Process tool gives you quick clarity, replacing fear or even soul-crushing mediocrity and even propels you back into loving life.

2. The Joy Scale helps you measure your progress in the realms of your life that are most important, so you can see exactly where you want to ignite your most impactful joy activators.

3. You will see what you are really committed to and how those commitments influence your current joy condition, so you can realign your choices, habits, and actions for greater joy.

4. You will begin to master being your own **joy expert** as you take yourself in new directions.

5. You'll learn what activates and de-activates your joy almost instantly.

Transitions and How to Use Them

I discovered an exciting connection between dreaming and navigating joy. When we are disconnected from joy, we also are disconnected from our dreams. Transitions can bring us closer to joy, or they can make us forget — forget about our dreams, aspirations, and who we really are.

> *Connect to joy, and you will connect (or re-connect) to your dreams!*

We are our transitions and the roles we assume inside each of them. When we are young, being alive is enough and joy is automatic. Then childhood quickly ends. We become teenagers, college students, get married, become parents, business owners, caregivers, etc. Each transition teaches us life lessons, including when to build up defenses. Fears and anxieties replace peace and joy. I say that joy is always available to us. However, with time, we get numb to it. Then we look for joy in many of the wrong places! Some of us forget joy until it's seemingly beyond us to experience it again.

Our transitions are filled with experiences we've never had and emotions we've never felt. We make choices before, during, and after each transition. Some of these choices bring lessons that, candidly, are hard on us and can even break us. However, I found that I needed these very lessons to learn how to break my heart open and activate joy! Some think of joy as child's play. I agree. But I don't think it's something we are required to grow out of. I think we forget how to get back to joy as we proceed through the various transitions that we all go through.

27

This book outlines and gives you the specific steps I discovered to recalibrate your actions and choices to align with your joy. In recalibrating, you'll discover you can navigate joy and up-level your own joy condition. I call that the G.P.S. to Joy.

It's All a Dance!

As a dancer, I see the transitions as the dances of our lives. Some dances we do with another, like the waltz; some with a group, like line dancing and folk dancing. Some dances are meant to be danced alone. In some dances, we follow, and in others, we lead. Most of the time, we are doing both, and that can lead to awkward stepping on toes at first.

> *Transitions and the turbulence they create hold the key to navigating your joy.*

How the steps and tempos change in the dances of a life intrigue me. We take on different roles and dance different tempos to varying beats as we move through transitions that make up life. And the music changes, often without us knowing.

Take a moment to envision yourself on the dance floor. Your dance partner? Joy. You may not know the exact steps but trust that dancing with joy will ultimately be worth the risk!

As you find your new rhythm, I know you will discover new steps that will take you in new directions. You will create a pathway to dance your way back to joy.

28

Connect to Joy

What is the Joy Activation Process?

The Joy Activation Process takes us on a journey using our most pressing challenges. It's a five-step process in which you explore these challenges and take on new actions to address them.

I created it as a method to take you from frustrated and stalled to having more power in your life and to activating your joy where it matters. The process invites new mindsets so you can upgrade and ignite joy again. By taking new actions from what you want now, you begin to navigate for more joy.

In the Joy Activation Process, start with a challenge to sink your teeth into. The most popular are:

1. Relationships
2. Career
3. Finances
4. Family & Parenting
5. Health and wellness
6. Community and friendships

Then ask...

1. **Step 1 – AWAKEN**
   Where is there room for more joy? What do you want that's different than what you have now? And why?

2. **Step 2 – ACKNOWLEDGE**
   What's the problem? What's off for you? Are you suffering something about it?

3. **Step 3 – ACT – NOW Action vs. NEW Action**
   Are your current actions moving you toward joy or away? What would you do instead, if anything?

4. **Step 4 – ADAPT**
   What adjustments would you be okay with making so that the new actions can stick? You need to allow for it to work!

5. **Step 5 – AFFIRM**
   Affirm it! And affirm yourself. Give yourself credit for taking a new action! See if it's working and adjust accordingly.

The Joy Navigator's Launch List

Every captain knows the equipment needed for the journey to go well. If you bring those things that shouldn't be on that list, the plane stays grounded or gets weighed down. Navigating joy is similar. Certain items properly equip the vessel or plane and other items are simply dead weight. Are you ready to be fully prepared for the launch?

Joy Navigation Launch List:

1. RELEASE EXCESS BAGGAGE like grudges, self-doubt, or resentments. You know that grudge you've had against your neighbor since VHS tapes were in vogue? If it doesn't elevate, you've got to eliminate. That includes approaches, mindsets, beliefs, and actions that are now obsolete. Let go

of whatever is no longer serving you so you don't get stalled or stuck in a tailspin. Let go so you can fly your new charted course and work around any turbulence.

2. <u>STOP BEING HYPER-CRITICAL</u> of yourself... of others. No one can be an effective co-captain if you don't give them the space to learn and grow. I call this making yourself a "no-bag" zone. Around you, no one can bag on themselves, i.e., diminish themselves in any way.

3. <u>HAVE A SOLID ROUTINE</u> to take care of your <u>mind, body, heart, and soul.</u> You have robust care rituals that keep the captain and vessel traveling smoothly! As a joy navigator, you know the importance of rest, of using great fuel, and how not to deplete your reserves.

4. <u>HAVE CONFIDENCE IN YOUR SKILLS.</u> You've got this. You know that on some level, life is inherently perfect as it is. You approach everyday with the confidence that nothing will stump you... you know I'm right!

5. <u>TRUST & BELIEVE IN YOURSELF</u>... all of you, especially the messy and vulnerable parts. You need every part of you to grow.

6. <u>YOU CAN SEPARATE THE CAPTAIN FROM THE VESSEL.</u> You have begun to unlink what you

do from the value of the human being that you hold, and you experience much more joy because of that.

7. YOU ARE 100% AWARE THAT YOU NEED NEW COORDINATES FOR YOUR NEW DIRECTION. You are it, the one responsible for your life and how you are doing. Your outcomes are yours and yours alone, and purposely, you fine tune as you go. You are growing, getting clearer and more aware about what best fuels you as you travel the new course you've charted.

8. YOU EMBODY JOY. It is a big part of you now. Because of that, people are pulled to you and can't help but contribute to you! You get smiles for no reason, and you might find that people in the grocery checkout line strike up conversations with you. You are a purveyor of joy!

9. YOU FLY IN THE DIRECTION YOU CHOOSE. You create your own happiness and you do work that fulfills you. You bring passion to your pursuits. You do what inspires you and delegate what draws down on your joy tank. You know how to stay balanced.

10. YOU HAVE THE COURAGE TO FLY FULL OUT. You really understand that your internal compass is guiding you and you listen to your intuition.

11. YOU SEEK YOUR OWN APPROVAL BECAUSE THAT'S ENOUGH NOW. You know your inherent value.

12. YOU RELEASE THAT WHICH WEIGHS YOU DOWN. You forgive yourself and others almost instantly. You're beyond aware of the emotions that ground you and the emotions that have you set you up for smooth sailing. You're done dwelling on the past. You do what's needed, take the steps, have the conversations, get closure, make new agreements, and do whatever you need to have emotional freedom. This sets you free. *"Forgiveness takes us off the wheel of suffering."* ~ *Marianne Williamson*

13. BOUNDARIES ARE SET, NO MATTER HOW WIDE. You have healthy boundaries that you maintain then re-draw as you change direction.

14. YOU HAVE CREATED A DELIBERATE PLAN. You live from intention and clear action from joy, not passive reaction.

15. YOU COURSE CORRECT FAST. If something is not working, you course correct as you keep moving forward.

Take a second look at the launch list and estimate your current position in relation to joy. If you could not see yourself in these scenarios – if you are living a far more turbulent life, that's okay. I'm going to help you course correct, so you can plan the coordinates and chart your path so that you can be prepared with only the equipment that you need.

Plotting Your Course to Joy

- Joy and dreams are intertwined. When you are disconnected from your dreams, the joy gap can be huge!
- Transitions are a normal part of living; however, sometimes transitions cause us to pull away from joy or to look for it in the wrong places.
- You can reconnect with and re-awaken the joy in your life in five steps – Awaken-Acknowledge-Act-Adapt-Affirm.
- No matter how turbulent your life might feel and seem right now, it's time to start navigating your joy.

Listen to what Maryl has to say about navigating joy at:
gpstojoybook.com

Chapter Three:

Straying from Joy: Your Tank on Empty

"Sometimes a simple shift in perspective is all you need to refocus your time and energy on what's important."
~ Melanie Benson

Imagine... you're having a conversation with joy.

"Hi, you! This is Joy talking. I've missed you! We always had so much fun together. I miss the sound of your laughter, the way you would dance in circles with your head back and your arms spread wide. We were tight! Two peas in a pod. What happened to you? Where did you go?! I'm still here. Last time I saw you, we were playing hide and seek. I hid. And waited... I'm still waiting. Why haven't you come back? I'm here, waiting for you in the sandbox, ready to play more! Where I am, the skies are blue, and we have a sacred bond filled with love and laughter. Many of us are back together on the playground beckoning you. Come find me again! I'm always here for you. Are you ready to come back? I promise I'll come take your hand when you call, *'Olly olly oxen free'*!"

Joy hasn't abandoned us, but through our turbulence and life's tough transitions, maybe we've forgotten joy. Maybe our joy tanks are simply sputtering empty. Let me share with you what took me from joy for a time.

At a young age, my brain sent me all kinds of un-encouraging and deflating messages. Maybe you know what I'm talking about. Even though I had a good head on my shoulders, I had the tendency to second guess myself by constantly wondering if I got it right. I'd then worry that I probably got it wrong. Or I would feel really bad. This negative habit came from a mindset I just didn't see. It was as if I had a war in my head between right and wrong, success and failure, being loved and being rejected. The inner conflict was exhausting! The thoughts in my head put me in a constant state of struggle. Damn, they seemed <u>so</u> real and became a big source of my suffering routine. Feeling bad, not knowing, messing it up… yada, yada, yada.

Notice anything about that paragraph?

My *mindset and interpretations* (my automatic reactions) caused my experience. My brain interpreted what was happening – fight or flight; emotions surfaced, including fear, worry, and feeling bad. My joy got trumped! And that's what often happens when we don't understand.

Take a second to reflect on how your reactions, thoughts, and mindsets steal your joy.

The Power of Mindset

Activating my joy brought to the surface for me mindsets and beliefs that had me stuck which then gave me the ability to replace them with alternative mindsets and beliefs around joy and abundance. Really! I wanted to have joy. Like a passionate kiss that continues for hours, I wanted to taste it, hear it, see it. Have it be so real that it felt like a rich chocolate truffle melting slowly on my tongue. Suffering repelled me the more I reconnected to joy.

I saw that we can adopt new mindsets because they are fluid. Consider lima beans and licorice. The thought of eating lima beans, to me, is like eating a crawling brown cricket. *Ugh*! Black Australian licorice, on the other hand, is like molten, sweet chocolate deliciously making its way from my tongue to my stomach. Now, if I were stranded on an island that only had lima beans, they would very quickly become my favorite food. And licorice would become a pleasant memory. The point: it's all in how we see it!

Our mindsets dictate the quality of our lives. They can free us or imprison us. Mindsets give us our choice to be joyful, separate from the situation, or to stay stuck. The choice is always ours.

So, are you ready for joy? Are you ready to uncover those things that light you up, like a passionate lover, wildflowers in bloom, fresh rain on your face, dancing naked in your bedroom, or having your finances seamlessly flowing?

> *Your mindset is your charted path either toward or away from joy.*

We choose the mindsets that take up residence in our heads. Transitions come. That's life. The hardest ones could easily break us. The opportunity for joy comes when we release our expectations and begin to see the transitions as "life happening," then simply let them be. Accepting the inherent perfection of life or letting them be is enough to soften the emotions of feeling let down. As I relax into the idea that everything that happens is perfect in ways that I may not understand, that allows me to relax a bit and let things be. There is a tight link between our need to control the uncontrollable and suffering. When I accept that reality, life gets easier and joy is right there.

The Roles We Play

We all have roles. Some flow easily and naturally with the rhythm of our lives. When our personal desires conflict with those roles, an unacknowledged longing can weigh on us. How many of us feel conflicted, questioning our choices, becoming weighed down by sadness and regret? Joy and satisfaction take a real beating then!

Our roles are pregnant with assumptions and expectations based on some ideal we feel driven to meet. We often take them on with gusto because they give us purpose. Our roles are beautiful! But they also ensnare us. The trap closes on us when we confuse giving value to being valuable. That steals joy!

We could allow ourselves to feel the sweetness that clarity of purpose gives by embracing those chosen roles. But, often we let the inner critic divert us. We start judging how we all measure up, using our roles to be hyper-demanding and hard on ourselves.

We are the sum total of our roles, experiences, commitments, disappointments, and movements that came before us. The qualities we bring to our worlds through our roles are infinite and evolutionary!

I think about the process we go through to integrate our true selves into our daily experiences as we perform our roles. I see navigating our joy and becoming our most authentic selves as simply consciously choosing every aspect of our lives, including our mindsets and beliefs. Daily, we can strengthen our muscle for *knowing* what we want and marrying that to a vision for *having* what we want.

Our roles, mindsets and beliefs adjust through each transition with their own unique lessons. I grew and matured from my lessons, like most of us. I also was tested, and when I failed in some way, I felt shame and got hard on myself. I began to feel unsafe and vulnerable, so I became hyper-vigilant to look out for future threats that might bring more shame. That was the beginning of my slide from joy.

When we are young, we're free spirits that love to play and be naturally interested in everything. Do you remember chasing lady bugs, petting caterpillars, and running naked in the rain? I do. I loved each moment. I believed that life was my giant playground.

Very quickly, transitions meant my fun would be disrupted. Big changes happened when more kids came into the family! My role changed to the understanding big sister who doesn't complain. My new belief morphed into: I am the oldest, and I need to be strong and smart.

The neighbor boy, Teddy, gave me my first kiss. I fell in love at the age of 4 and believed that every day was filled with excitement when someone loves you. Then, Teddy's family moved. I never saw them leave. Around that same time, my caregiver, the woman who felt more like a mom, also left unexpectedly. Right then, I started to believe that people I love leave, so I wanted to protect myself and not become so attached. I took on the role of being independent and careful.

We've all worn many hats and played many roles and attached beliefs and expectations to each of them. Mine included:

1. Being a stellar student (belief: performance gets you approval.)

2. Being a good soldier (belief: not making waves gets you love.)

3. Being ambitious (belief: you need to be independent to survive.)

4. Being an entrepreneur (belief: I can only depend on myself to financially thrive.)

5. Being a good citizen (belief: you are only as valuable as your latest contribution.)

6. Being a diligent daughter, wife and mother (belief: being a woman of value includes getting married, having children and caring for parents.)

7. Becoming a divorcee (belief: there is no safe relationship. I'm a failure at intimate love and I can only depend on myself to protect myself and my child.)

8. Becoming a doctor's wife (belief: I will be a woman of value with a husband of prestige. Then I can be extraordinary if he is.)

9. Being a caregiver to my aging parents (belief: I'm the strong one and you can count on me to care for others' needs over my own because they are more important.)

10. Being a young widow (belief: the people you love eventually leave. Love always carries pain.)

11. Being a great friend (belief: the way to have people stick around is to be the best friend you can be and suck it up.)

12. Being nice (belief: setting boundaries separates me from people I love. I can't disappoint or I will lose critical connections.)

The list goes on. It's designed to shed light on the interplay between our roles, our beliefs, and our expectations. Beliefs give us the playbook for how we execute our roles. Expectations give us the playbook for why. As I allowed my beliefs and mindsets to mature, I uncovered the expectations I was living from. I also learned that self-care is a stepping stone back to joy. The tests and trials of the many roles can take us down the path to what authentically gives us joy.

When the Joy Tank is Empty

Anything can give us power when we let it. Mostly, we react to survive. You've heard of being in survival mode. It's a common fall back. For a long time, survival mode was habitual for me. My instincts would turn me into a control junkie, where I lived in constant alert and believed the only way to fend off danger was to control my environment. I added more armor to my heart, hired more attorneys for my business, and put distance between me and others. My primary goal was to find something I could control or, at a minimum, avoid the shame of failure. I had to execute things perfectly to survive! This approach to everything took me away from joy and ultimately served to empty my joy tank.

I became aware of so much that empties our joy tanks, like:

- Imposing expectations.
- Believing that we are falling short.
- Treating my roles as an imposition or an annoying obligation instead of seeing them as opportunities for growth, to serve others, and to show love.

- Focusing on staying safe by avoiding danger or a state of confusion.
- Letting our compulsions and anxieties drive us and our actions.
- Staying quiet to keep peace over truth; avoiding confrontation at the expense of voicing what needs to be voiced.
- Stifling emotions.
- Being hard on ourselves as a matter of course.

I don't know about you, but when I let my fight-or-flight reactions go on auto-pilot, joy takes a back seat and my ability to consciously choose vanishes for that moment!

Since joy is a choice, what stops us from staying connected to it? What allows us to drain our joy tanks and stay on empty? There could be a million reasons why. The biggest culprit? Coaching has shown that to be an internal conflict that's under the surface which resides where we can't see. So we suffer it or deal with it or find some way to cope with not having what we truly want.

> *Care for yourself first or you will be unable to fulfill any other role in your life.*

We regularly put others' needs before our own. We are created to do that. But then we get so burdened by the demands of our roles that tending to ourselves turns into an afterthought... that is until our bodies get pushed to a breaking point or some other crisis causes a change.

The belief that caring for ourselves can't happen when we have other major responsibilities is not factual. We can bring a new point of view to this equation. We need to awaken to a new view of our roles and add a role in which we are the primary driver of our own care. Without doing so, your joy tank will remain empty!

If we simply ask ourselves, "What brings me joy," how would we redirect ourselves? What mindset adjustments or shifts to our beliefs could we bring to our roles, so we could mature our life into an experience of thriving?

Are there habits or beliefs that have us suffer more than enjoy? Could we let go of the ones that keep us stuck?

Plotting Your Course to Joy

- Joy never leaves us; instead, we tend to stray from it.
- Your mindset and beliefs are incredibly powerful. They can either lead you toward or away from joy. The choice is yours.
- You have many roles over the course of your life, and navigating your joy means gaining the ability to consciously choose every aspect of your life.
- Your survival-mode mindsets and beliefs can lock you into suffering and interfere with your experience and connection with joy.

Listen to what Maryl has to say about navigating joy at:
gpstojoybook.com

Chapter Four

Habits that Get Us Off Course

"Your net worth to the world is usually determined by what remains after your bad habits are subtracted from your good ones." ~ Benjamin Franklin

For a long time, I had a chronic habit of jumping in and out of life's frying pans. I put myself in hot water, then wonder why it hurts so much! I would solve one crisis, only to have another one pop up so that I could take all the necessary steps to solve that one, too, even if it was not my crisis to solve! Same fire, different pans.

This can be a good trait—having a reliable capacity to solve problems. The problem was that I wasn't really satisfied when the crisis ended. There was no joy… just an urgent need to find the next fire to jump into. I did this in many ways, and it looked like I was making "choices." Then I discovered that this was actually the way I was conditioned to lead my life. I complicated matters by assuming the issues of others—and they weren't mine to solve. My boundaries were blurry.

I attribute this habit – one that steered me away from joy – to being the oldest child in my family where I was rewarded for being responsible. Our family had its issues, like any family. To me, it seemed like our family life was constantly in a frying-pan-to-fire situation. My modus operandi was to try to fix every situation. But I was a child, so I couldn't really fix problems that big. So, with time, I sought out situations in life that I could fix.

My ambition to do everything perfectly had me failing constantly, since perfection is an illusion. The sensible me wanted to play it safe and stay out of harm's way. Yet, I continued to migrate to the messiest of messes. The result? I was being slow cooked by my choices. It took the heat's constant rising for me to eventually notice this powerful conditioning. As you can imagine, *joy* doesn't fit in the frying-pan-to-the-fire equation.

When I looked deeper at why I had taken up this habit, I saw that this was how I felt most alive! My heart pounded like a beating drum and I could feel my blood pumping through my veins. It was adrenaline, not joy. I felt smart and relevant every time I successfully solved a crisis and removed myself from another hot mess. The catch was that no sooner would I handle a giant problem than another spark of chaos would start to burn with a new fire. It was primal and addictive – adrenaline is. It kept me going, but not by navigating my joy.

> *Do not confuse adrenaline (although it can be energizing) for joy.*

I put myself into these unsettling situations in a multitude of ways. In college, I picked men that were good for fun but not for long-term, healthy relationships. I'd dive in and throw caution to the wind. Shortly thereafter, my heart would be broken.

With men and business, I was naïve and overly trusting way too soon, being lured by whoever gave me attention or who would give me any love at all. I acted impulsively from a desperate place. What I needed to do was slow down and ask myself what I wanted, what would serve me... but I was way off course.

My first husband was not an easy partner for me. Everyone involved, including the families, were impacted by our marital dramas. I had married someone for the possibility of who he could be, and I thought love would handle our difficulties.

In my business, I was constantly on edge because our production was frequently in flux. I became a master at managing this edge. Even with an amassed business savings, I wasn't prepared for the necessary downsizing when the economy tanked and my supply route was suddenly halted due to the SARS virus outbreak in China.

Running the business had been tax year to tax year, not unlike someone living paycheck to paycheck. The adrenaline rush was addicting. I was used to the struggle, and that gave me a story to tell. No joy there!

Even with David, my late husband, I was blindly "all in," even when his commitment seemed lukewarm. I remained in emotional flux over eight years before getting clear that we were both on the same page about marriage and life partnership. Staying with him in flux taxed me and was a risk to my long-term happiness because I was still in my childbearing years and wanted the option to have more children.

Waiting that length of time spent me. We had a push-and-pull dynamic that tired us both. Being in flux for so long had me question my worthiness and my lovability. I continued far too long in this struggle to stay relevant, desperate to feel deserving of his love as a life mate.

The root cause of questioning my worthiness for love was due to my view that life, love, and business had to be dramatic and difficult. The struggle, hidden from my view for many years, had me feel more alive, relevant, and loved because I had done the work to earn it!

Finally, the time came for me to stand up and speak up for what I needed with my parents and with David. Something shifted for me, almost like an internal, heart-centered recalibration. In simple terms, I gained more self-love and personal compassion that fueled the courage to directly voice my needs. Life eased up, and I had more compassion for others, too. As I was there for myself, I could be more there for others. My heart now knew a new level of personal trust, and I relaxed knowing that I could have a rich and peaceful life without the catalyst of a crisis. It finally hit me! Love and ease were no longer things I needed to fight for. I could trust myself and simply allow for them to emerge.

The day came when I saw that I did not have to jump through hoops to get approval and be loveable. My worthiness was no longer in question. I didn't have to sizzle inside of every frying pan or fire to prove my value. Wonderful experiences came my way over time: David and I married, I experienced more friendships and deeper love, I bought a house and a building, and I wrote this book and so much more.

Finding Strength to Course Correct

I still have knee-jerk thoughts in the back of my overachieving mind that I could have done more, been more, given more, but I do my best to **not** indulge them.

Experiencing joy has now replaced my previous thirst for adrenaline. In fact, joy is my new baseline. As part and parcel to that, I create intentions, embrace visions for how my life unfolds, and I experience dreams consciously fulfilled.

At the end of their lives, it was important to me that both my parents and David had peaceful endings. This could have been a dramatic undertaking, just another frying pan. Instead, I brought vision and intention to the process and did my utmost to ensure that it wasn't detrimental to any of us. I did some serious inner work and focused on my growth through these transitions. I created joy as I could. I knew witnessing their passings would be painful but also a privilege. My capacity to bring intention and compassion to even the toughest experiences allowed for more love than suffering. Rather than avoiding the painful emotions, I made room for all of the emotions that arose for all of us in dealing with death, without judgment of anyone, including myself. When I felt weak, my community stepped in with love and support that elevated all of us.

After all three of my loved ones passed on, I got quiet and asked my whole self what it would take for me to rise above my broken heart. Year one after David died, my mandate was clear – don't die of a broken heart. Yet I had no idea how to do that. I found myself creating this mantra: no drama and don't get stuck. I took time to meditate on the question: "How can I repair a heart that's been so painfully broken open?" My god, everything in me hurt! So that question was a good first step. My focus shifted from the crisis "out there" to what was happening "over here" within... from solving crises for other people to restoring and caring for myself.

At this point, I don't have drama and I don't get stuck very often. I still do feel nervous or uncomfortable from time to time, but I don't put myself in crisis modes of not knowing where my next meal is coming from, or obsessing about whether my relationship will work out, or putting myself in financial stress in my businesses. I take much better care of myself now in every realm that is important to me.

Use Your Strengths

Here are tips on using your own strengths for finding solutions that will allow you to navigate your joy:

- After you use your ability to deal effectively with a crisis, please don't create another one. Give yourself a moment to see and appreciate how capable you are. Let the joy sink in.
- Create a mantra that speaks to you that you can call on anytime. My favorite is: No drama, and don't get stuck.
- Use your strengths to find solutions that work for you. Think, do, and be whomever you need to so that you stop suffering the intolerable.
- When you find yourself in the midst of turbulence (inner or outer), interrupt that experience by taking time for yourself, be compassionate, and allow for all your emotions. They will flow through you if you don't stop them.
- Appreciate yourself, your abilities, and what you bring to others.

- When you feel like you are failing or suffering, let your community help you carry the load. Trust that loving kindness is always there.

I took deep joy in who I was for my family and what I facilitated for their endings. I appreciated my capacities, my attitude and my mastery of the diplomacy involved to solve issues before they became a Herculean crisis. I acknowledged the fun I could bring in and how I could move people in a way that would serve the greater good. To my surprise, I didn't need medication to stabilize. I had taken on personal growth and transformational studies for several years, which empowered me. Through it all, I could see how I developed my strength and abilities without resorting to crisis management mode.

I'm sure I'll continue to solve big problems and continue to help people because both of those things bring me joy. *G.P.S. to Joy* is a more mature version of it. I'll continue because it's my dream that people choose joy and loving connection over struggle and suffering.

I have elevated what makes me relevant to me, my family, my community. My aim now is that you will elevate and grow to navigate your joy right along with me.

Plotting Your Course to Joy

- After you use your ability to deal effectively with a crisis, please don't create another one. Interrupt that habit.
- Find your own mantra and use it to help break any debilitating addiction you might have.

- Use your strengths to find solutions to consciously generate what you want.
- When you manage a situation, take time for yourself, be compassionate, and allow for all your emotions to flow.
- Take time to reflect and appreciate yourself, your abilities, and what you bring to others.
- When you feel like you are failing or weak, **let** your community in to support you. The key to having a great outcome is to surround yourself with people who deeply care.

Listen to what Maryl has to say about navigating joy at:
gpstojoybook.com

Part 2: Plotting New Coordinates

"Nothing comes ahead of its time, and nothing has ever happened that didn't need to happen." ~ *Byron Katie*

It's time to start plotting new coordinates so that you can fully navigate your joy. If you're reluctant to reposition—to find new stars by which to guide your own course—I get that. Been there, done that as I've shared in the first part.

Honestly, you have two choices: Remain stalled right where you are (and I assure you, you will never find joy there) or plot new coordinates and decide to become the navigator and captain of your life and the joy that you can uncover and revel in.

You must first relax, let go a bit, and get beyond your previous line of sight because you can no longer navigate by that. Only when you let go of the past can you course correct to a joyful future. Your roles have changed, so it's time to discover your new true north. Conditions may be shrouded in fog at the moment, so I want to help you gain the clarity you need to intentionally reposition. It's work I've done as a coach to help countless men and women navigate their joy and move forward toward wonderful new horizons.

Plotting New Coordinates

Chapter Five:

Filling Your Joy Tank

We've looked at how easy it is to turn away from joy—the kind of joy that lightness brings. We've talked about joy from several angles, including how our attitudes and beliefs about our roles and responsibilities can make or break our joy. We've talked about the havoc expectations wreak when they infiltrate our relationships and how we see life! We also explored how we can derail ourselves and keep ourselves in survival mode when we correlate what we do and how "well" we do it with our intrinsic value. If I could, I'd completely outlaw **that** practice!

So, how can we navigate joy when it seems like it's gone silent—when your joy tank is empty? First, consider these joy fundamentals:

- Joy is a choice that is both passive and active.
- It can come to us spontaneously!
- It can also come from having the conscious intention to create joy.
- Joy always lives inside the potential of our imagination, our dreams and our vision.
- Joy takes practice, like meditation or yoga. And the practicing is a gateway to our joy connection as we fine tune your ability to feel it.
- Although joy is as universal as smiling, it's still individual to each of us and definitely has us feeling alive and connected.

Let's start unpacking these fundamentals of joy to provide you with a new perspective and new coordinates that will enable you to chart a new path—an intentional one and one that will allow you to make joy a priority in your life.

> *You can only navigate joy when you understand and embrace the fundamentals.*

First, joy feeds on lightness as in "lightening up," like an Oprah or Deepak kind of lightening up. How many times do your closest people say, "You know, you are really intense. Get out of your head and lighten up! Have some fun, laugh! Chill!" This was essentially my late husband's daily message to me.

To lighten up takes letting things go, especially those emotions, fears and feelings that make us miserable. When we release those emotions, it's virtually impossible to stay in the shadows of self-consciousness and deep worry. Often, our hearts open. People who I've mentored and coached tell me that when they get lighter, they attract people to them effortlessly and don't feel alone. Joy seems to sneak right in!

Joy also likes us to ask questions and shift how we see things. I have discovered that it is a kind of art. The art comes from developing the skill in asking questions that bring options to the issue at hand. That is the essence of the Joy Activation Process. There is a bonus when we ask without rushing to conclusions. Answers come that give us room to breathe and progress.

Joy needs dreams of all shapes and sizes. Like asking questions in new ways, dreaming is a muscle of the soul and strengthens with use. The more we dream, the more our lives take on the flavors we relish most.

Joy needs something big to attach to, a fundamental reason why. Why? Because only a big enough reason gets us to go to the other side of accepting the status quo and staying in our safe zones and away from things that get uncomfortable—when the waters get rough and turbulent. Of course, getting outside our comfort zone happens when we embark on something new. We can count on our innate safety mechanisms to interfere with our actions to up-level our lives when things show up that are alien to us.

Joy needs unyielding compassion that's stronger than our negativity. I call that being a no-bag zone. Inside this zone, we don't bag on ourselves or others. We give less air time to our fears, anxieties, and compulsions and listen more to the part of us that dreams and strives to feel more alive than ever. We become a safe space for ourselves and others that's free from diminishment. Being a no-bag zone is another way to describe cultivating a habit where we affirm and uplift ourselves and each other and embrace the failures that guide us to new paths.

Joy calls for us to upgrade our habits, like being present and mindful or acting from love.

Joy needs us to interrupt patterns that stop joy—like softening our natural tendency to be right or adjusting where we tend to get over-the-top invested in anyone or anything. I'll be the first to admit that meeting this particular need of joy is challenging. From time to time, I still find myself literally addicted to needing to know, not letting go, and being right (my daughter will confirm this!). I can tell when I'm having an episode of "know-it-all-itis" when I buy the party-sized bag of chocolate kisses and eat them all. Overdosing on chocolate is my signal that there is something for me to grow through that will allow me to release habits that keep me stuck like a butterfly in cement.

Joy shows up in our communities. Anything we need to navigate even our hardest transitions is there. And our communities go beyond the neighborhood. The online world has really changed that! Whether it's my neighbor or my Facebook community, we will always find people who have walked our specific path before us. When we embrace our communities, we are never alone.

Joy thrives on our vows and commitments.

Joy grows with trust, starting with ourselves and expanding from there. I'm not talking about blind trust. I'm referring to the sort of trust where we see clearly what we can trust ourselves and others for, then counting on them for those things. I contend (and my coaching clients will agree) that one big way you can trust me is with big problems. Almost without question, you can trust me to uncover and facilitate a powerful solution quickly... a solution that enables joy navigation. What is it that people trust about you? Take a few moments to really consider this question as the answer is very likely one of the coordinates you need to chart your new path.

Joy needs us to speak up so that our voice does not get hijacked by our inner chatter telling us to just stay quiet. With the people I love, I tell them when I'm feeling vulnerable. I tell them what I'm feeling that's more than a passing thought, so they know what's going on with me. Nothing comes between us. When I need support, I ask for it and they provide it. We support each other, especially when huge uncertainties surface. When we simply listen, it's amazing how most issues lose their grip! Withholding what is going on with us is a way to hide ourselves that saps our joy energy.

Similarly, joy soars when we know what we need, want, and yearn for. Without that clarity, it is much harder to know when we are in our joy.

Joy needs contrast. Without some difficulty or pain, discerning authentic joy and pleasure is harder to see. Experiencing the difference lets us truly know joy.

There are maintenance tasks or inner housekeeping chores involved in keeping joy present.

Navigating joy entails:

- Decluttering
- Getting clear on what brings you joy
- Opening yourself up to new avenues for having joy
- Expanding and evolving how you see things to let more joy in
- Opening your hearts
- Being present
- Building solid self-care practices
- Updating healthy boundaries for yourself
- Affirming yourself and others
- Refraining from diminishing anyone
- Trusting your worthiness
- Taking loving actions
- Being a joy explorer

Our joy tanks overflow when we act from love and when we trust the process. And, yes, as we begin, we need to act without a clear roadmap. We need to be willing to not know precisely what lies ahead. We really don't "know" anything anyway. Only a few of us are fortune tellers who can predict the future. I found that letting go of being right or being overly vested moves mountains!

Let me say: I still love to control where I can. I also find myself lured by knowing and using willpower to maneuver things to go my way. Almost like swimming in mud! But, when I'm clear that's fruitless, I relax.

> *You can only control your mindset and your actions... nothing else.*

What we can control is what we imagine, dream, and envision. From those, we can take new actions, which is both frightening and awesome.

Joy came to me when I finally made peace with the fact that in general, I have control over three things: my mindset, my choices, and my actions. Seeing this freed me up and I spend much less energy where it won't help anyway.

Fuel for Joy

We've talked about navigating joy. Does joy need nurturing, too? I say yes. But how? What nourishes joy and our being?

A thirst for discovery, taking stock, embracing stillness, connecting to community, letting go, plugging into divine energy, cultivating self-awareness and self-confidence, self-compassion, and self-care. It's endless!

Here are some other considerations for nourishing joy that might surprise you:

1. Transitions. They let us reinvent!
2. Internal conflicts. They aid us in our journey to joy.
3. The shifts we make when we integrate ourselves... when we move from sacrificing to celebrating and taking care of ourselves.
4. Courage. To challenge the thoughts and emotions that interfere with joy.
5. Baby steps. Breaking down issues and circumstances to bring a fresh view to them.
6. Responding mindfully, not simply reacting – which happens when we manage our anxieties, fears, and compulsions that can often drive us.
7. Patience: A very wise therapist told me, "You can't get to spring until the winter ends. It comes in its time."
8. Trusting and accepting things as they are. This includes people!
9. Compassion and the gentle release of the power we give our preconceptions and pre-judgments.
10. Clarifying the many roles we've played through each transition. Choosing and unfolding our new roles, including gaining insight into what feeds our joy.
11. Learning what fuels our enthusiasm and vibrancy and sharing that with people. Getting that same information from them!
12. Shifting from unconsciously acting and expecting to actively defining what we want together with others.

13. Reflecting — noticing when we are connected to joy and keeping that connection alive.
14. Asking, "What brings me joy?" Then embracing the answers and putting them to work!
15. Imagination and dreaming!

C.S. Lewis wrote, "Real joy seems to me almost as unlike security or prosperity as it is unlike agony…. It jumps under one's ribs and tickles down one's back and makes one forget meals and keeps one (delightedly) sleepless o' nights. It shocks one awake when the other puts one to sleep. My private table is one second of joy is worth 12 hours of pleasure.

"Joy (in my sense) has indeed one characteristic, and one only, in common with them; the fact that anyone who has experienced it will want it again…. I doubt whether anyone who has tasted it would ever, if both were in his power, exchange it for all the pleasures in the world."

Joy is always inviting its presence and is available to experience. It is not forced. Choice is our access to joy. Our willingness to have joy is also essential. The condition of joy is much more powerful than our desire to control, command, or force it.

Exercise: Are You Ready for Joy?

To proceed, are you a resounding, "Yes! I'm all in?" Will you:

- Shift from controlling and try simply relaxing into things?
- Accept yourself, others and circumstances as they are versus what you want them to be?

- Dream again?
- Experience joy like never before?
- Embrace your quirky humanness — the good, the bad, and the messy — and then do the same for others?
- Navigate your joy by dismantling some of your hard edges and ushering light into the cracks of your heart?

I'm all in, too, so let's start measuring and igniting the joy that we deserve!

Plotting Your Course to Joy

- Joy is fundamental, like the air we breathe.
- Joy has many things it needs in order to be present.
- Joy needs to be fed, and feeding and fueling it allows it to multiply.
- Inner work chores navigate joy.
- Get ready to turn on your JOY ignition!

Listen to what Maryl has to say about navigating joy at:
gpstojoybook.com

Filling Your Joy Tank

Chapter Six:

The Joy of Navigating Your Finances

Let's face it. We all know money isn't everything. But without it, we can feel like we are drowning. When we're in those "Holy Crap! I'm broke!" moments, joy is hard to come by.

In navigating my own joy, I found that getting back on my feet financially was, again, like dancing. I started by moving forward ever so slightly, and I took one step at a time. Then another. My ability to make good choices improved, and my results shifted after I made it a point to learn about the steps I needed to take to have healthy finances.

One of the cold-water-in-my-face moments came in May 2001, when I had just purchased a home.

When I left a marriage that wasn't working five years earlier, I had no real idea of what I was going to do. I was a 33-year-old single mom with an infant. Then my parents took us in for four years and gave us unconditional love, for which I am eternally grateful.

With that purchase, I finally had a home where I could raise my daughter in peace without constant wrangling over custody or critical comments from my mother (to be fair, we had completely interrupted her peaceful retirement).

So there I was as I lay in bed in my new, charming, 1954 dream house. And I was freezing my butt off! It was drafty, and I couldn't get warm with the one blanket I owned!

Now what?

All I could do was cry. I was confronted by the reality that I could not afford another blanket. I was in over my head financially, and I was humiliated. I never would have imagined that humiliation was what I would feel in that moment. I thought I'd feel euphoric! I was finally free!

What was needed now was brutal honesty with myself. What had driven me to marry the man I had? What did I need to learn now from all of it—the roller coaster marriage, the roller coaster divorce, the roller coaster business, the roller coaster finances? How could I get off the roller coaster and stabilize my finances and begin to love life?

> *I could not begin to navigate my own joy until I learned to navigate my financial footing.*

Taking a candid view of my situation, I confronted myself with hard facts and questions. There was drama everywhere. I was a stroke waiting to happen! My anxiety had never been higher.

My finances had really suffered from being in family court every quarter. I was still afraid of my ex-husband's demands and rarely got a full night's sleep. My heart broke daily because of the toll it was taking on all involved, especially my child.

Living on my own with a house in my name should bring me joy, right? Instead, I was freezing to the bone with no blankets, and I had a significant mortgage. I was living paycheck to paycheck. I thought none of that would matter. After all, I had endured a lot. Now I had a corner lot with three tall trees in the front yard. I ought to be in heaven with a new baseline for joy, but I wasn't. Not at first, anyway.

There were other stages I needed to experience before peace and freedom were mine. I already knew that the lottery is not a financial plan, a man is not a plan, and luck is not a plan. So, I shifted my mindset to be responsible. I knew I could do this. I *would* get my financial house in order.

If an emergency of any kind, like a major car repair or a sudden need to move came along, I'd be in dire straits. I needed coupons to be able to buy anything, including toilet paper. I felt alone, and I didn't reach out for help because of my ego. I could handle a crisis, couldn't I? I could do it all on my own, couldn't I?

One of the first things I did was admit to people who cared about me that I needed help. More importantly, I allowed them to be there for me. I found myself being thankful, checking my ego, and putting a stop to my "I've got to do it all myself or I am worthless" inner critic.

Humiliation turned into humility. I had to admit to myself that I was financially undereducated. I was humbled that neighbors would make me dinner; humbled that they were willing to give me some blankets; humbled that I allowed them to help me and they allowed me to help them. It became easy, a heartfelt give and take. I was willing to be understanding and to accept myself. I matured from humiliation and arrogance and became accepting — of myself, of giving and of receiving.

Then I'd say, "Hey, who's got some blankets? Listen, who's got dinner tonight? I'll get it tomorrow night." I didn't have to be perfect anymore. I could just ask for help. I grew in my appreciation for people's love and generosity and vowed to give back. I began to experience a whole other side to friendship and community. Mutually caring and helping each other replaced my fears of not being able to handle life alone. And I stopped needing to go primal and isolate myself to avoid embarrassment. I let go of my pride and gave up the pressure of having to be a superstar. I let other people in.

I began to find ideas and answers from several sources. I talked to people about how they made ends meet as single parents. I applied for scholarships for camps and sports activities that were beyond the budget. I looked for out-of-the-box solutions.

Then I took a hard look at my financial priorities. I wanted to ensure my daughter would have money for education and big life events should I die or be disabled. I also learned about organizing for later years and retirement. I bought a small life insurance policy for my daughter's benefit. I started a savings account. I'd look at it once a week. My goal was to live within and below my means and to look at new ways to bring in income.

I became mature about finances and gained mastery as a single mom and owner of a business. I learned the value of prioritization. Here is the checklist of my financial priorities to bring me joy that comes from peace of mind.

My Financial Joy Checklist:
1. Health insurance
2. Savings for college and daily living
3. Retirement funding
4. Life insurance
5. Disability insurance

6. Negotiation for reductions in debt

What is your checklist? What would it take for you to have financial joy?

Assess for yourself how well you work with finances on a scale of 1 to 10. Your answer:

_____

<1=I'm broke   10=I have financial joy>

What tools or resources do you have, or could you find, for budgeting, debt review, planning and saving, and setting goals for yourself and your family?

Are there benefits and educational resources that you have because of your affiliations, for example, with your bank and credit card company, with your credit union, at your local community center, from military benefits, and the like?

Do you have an accountant or CPA or bookkeeper friend who can direct you?

To achieve financial stability, I had to want a different outcome with finances. I had to be willing to learn and not beat myself up. I really lightened up and let help in. At long last, I got more real with myself and stopped the disabling self-judgment. I didn't have to be perfect. I just had to start.

Taking the First Steps

Here are some beginning steps I took to get stronger on my financial feet.

Write it down: Income flow, fixed expenses, variable expenses, savings, credit card pay down, upcoming vacations, other expenses.

Put it in a spreadsheet and update it monthly. I have this information in a financial application on my computer so I can see everything now.

Learn: You can get a free education from bank and credit card websites.

Talk to people in the financial industry who you know to further educate yourself and get direction where you need it.

For bigger ticket purchases, talk with someone who can provide advice. For example, I check with my CPA for her recommendation on how and when to buy them.

Plan for and save for retirement with consistency. Again, there are many websites and resources to move you forward on this today.

Some key questions to answer to gain solid footing in your finances:

1. Does your work (or ability to earn income) light you up and bring you joy?

2. How long do you see yourself filling that role at work?

3. Are you balanced in your income and expenses now?

4. How much do you need to live on?

5. Do you have goals and dreams that you want to put money toward?

6. How can that happen?

7. When you are 65, would you live differently and how would you like your finances to be at that point?

These questions do not need immediate answers. However, I propose them to get you on your way toward navigating financial joy! Like any dance, you won't know the best way to take the step until you try it. Eventually, the dance will come together, and you will have the skills to up-level your finesse with your finances. It's a process, and the accomplishments inside the problems can raise your confidence and give you joy as you establish solid financial footing.

As I answered the questions, I figured out how to fund my home, handle emergencies and unexpected expenses, get an easy-to-follow retirement funding plan started, funding college—including the myriad scholarships that are available for anybody—and more. It took several years to bring vision and results to this realm.

I shifted my thinking. I went from, "I like that skirt, I'll buy it," to seeing when, how and if it makes sense to buy it. As I learned to live fully awake to my finances and my financial goals, I had to get creative so I could stay on track. I found cool consignment stores and people I could trade with. We used the library for videos and audio books. I saw what I needed versus wanted and had a bigger vision that took me beyond **that** skirt.

I developed patience. I gained more gratitude. I had much more compassion for people dealing with the financial aspects of life, and many others. That has been worth its weight in gold!

If you are interested in being introduced to financial finesse **for free**, check out the following ways to get educated:

- Courses on Udemy
- Courses on Coursera (recommended by Forbes)
- YouTube videos on financial literacy
- Financial experts, Suze Orman and Dave Ramsey have a variety of programs for anyone at any stage of learning
- Can you think of anyone to talk to in your neighborhood, community or church/place or worship that can give you quick direction?

I created a plan that started with taking an honest assessment of my financial circumstances. I sought out education from a financial advisor. To begin, I spoke to small, local financial planning firms. I found Edward Jones advisors to be very patient and beyond helpful. They helped with budgeting, insurance, savings, and how to see money in a new way. I noticed they were willing to help everyone from novices to veteran investors. They gave me more resources for retirement planning, so I was able see the whole of it. I sought out the education and found an abundance of it!

I grounded myself in what it took to be responsible for my financial world, today and well into the future. That effort and the requisite actions allowed me to create independence, freedom… and joy!

I have found there's joy in developing compassionate and practical practices for having financial finesse! After 30 years of this practice, I am now semi-retired. I purchased another home, and I invest to have passive income in my retirement.

All of this happened by shifting how I saved and spent, and how I took responsibility for my financial life. I found joy in growing my ability to navigate finances.

Plotting Your Course to Joy

- Get deeply connected to your income and expenses as they are today as your starting point.
- Create your financial joy checklist, so you have a focus.
- Ask key questions that will show you where to up-level your financial education.
- Study financial fundamentals using the free resources that are on the internet, in the library, and within your community and financial institutions.
- Ground yourself and give yourself the patience and time to develop your financial growth and development.
- The sooner you begin, the better. The fact is that you'll have expanded results the more time you give yourself.

Listen to what Maryl has to say about navigating joy at: gpstojoybook.com

Chapter Seven:

The Joy Scale

"Find a place inside where there's joy, and the joy will burn out the pain." ~ *Joseph Campbell*

Life's defining moments—you know which ones... those light bulb moments that permanently change the course of our lives. These are what I call transitions.

Others call them losses or passages. Whatever you call them, they share some common features. First, we often don't see them coming. Second, they are definitely life-altering. Third, they hit us hard like a tidal wave, a blow so potent that nothing we know to be true seems to remain in its aftermath.

With the old terrain gone, we are left completely exposed, dazed, and blinded in our ability to see what's next. Only then can transformation begin. Only when we admit we are lost can we take the steps needed to find new direction. Something very subtle, beyond our consciousness, goes to work and sharpens our ability to navigate these transitions. In that instant, that transition demands our attention and requires us to expand and unfold new ways of being. We have no option but to slow down and take on new practices and insert a new kind of intention into our choices. This gives way to upgrades in our perspective. We start creating instead of reacting. We begin to navigate joy, giving our soul's voice more of a say. Controlling through sheer willpower gives way. New mindsets emerge, allowing us to refine our choices and actions.

I am acutely aware of how easy it is to lose our connection to what brings us joy. When that happens, it's time for a serious disruption. That's why I created the Joy Activation Process. It fuels you to power up your joy, turn on your dream ignition, and begin to plot out a new reality.

Joy has a wide spectrum — it can come spontaneously, and it can be sustained. Sustained joy needs more from us. We must activate it by becoming more aware of what's true for us, connecting to that truth, and by simple practice.

When we hone in on we want and connect to what's important to us, then we activate joy.

Walking among giant trees like the sequoias in California brings me unadulterated joy. They're majestic! What I most appreciate is what each tree endures to experience massive growth! As saplings, they are vulnerable and exposed to the elements. Over time, they grow to a point where even fires can't burn them down. In fact, fires renew them!

Their root systems are even more interesting. The roots get nourished by seeking out roots of other trees, then binding with them. The connectedness formed by the bond lets them all grow stronger and taller and is vital for their existence.

Like living, breathing trees, our joy and our beings need to be nourished. As with trees, we sprout branches that are akin to the realms of our lives. Our branches grow leaves which come and eventually drop off, which I see as the matters and issues we mature through and the transitions that take us there. We are both nurtured and challenged by the elements. Some days we face storms and turbulence. Other days, we have blue skies. Each element helps us thrive, and when fires confront us, we can trust that we will be renewed.

Every captain or pilot has a pre-launch checklist. Before they leave the tarmac or the dock, this checklist is reviewed. Each item, every time. The checklist is a constant for them. They leave nothing to chance. Similarly, they never set out on a new course until they are certain they know where they are at the moment. A firm starting point is key to successful navigation.

> *You must have honest clarity about where you are right now before you can navigate toward joy.*

How can we track our joy condition? How can we know our starting point? The Joy Scale gives you a real-time read on your experience of joy in each area of your day-to-day life. The structure of the Joy Scale has us assign values to each realm. The more detailed you are, the clearer your results and progress. Now, on to the Joy Scale!

Realms and Their Challenges

Each of us has distinct realms that are personally most important. Where there's a realm, there could be a challenge or issue to deal with. When you take a look at the Joy Scale, you'll see that the most common realms are there. Modify or add to them as you want.

Remember that prioritization allows you to better navigate joy. First, you'll rank the realms by importance. That will help you select the top three on which to focus. If you're not sure right away, a good place to start is with those areas that weigh on you, where you feel stuck, or where there isn't good flow.

Rank each one on a scale of 1 to 10, with 1 being least important right now and 10 being most important. While each of these realms is important, you'll pare your focus down to three that are important **now**.

I encourage you to repeat this exercise and apply the Joy Activation Process to any realm you choose. For now, focus on no more than three because shifts are incremental and navigating joy is a process. Addressing too many at once can be self-defeating.

Here are the most common realms and examples of universal challenges that will help you recognize and prioritize your top three:

___ Realm 1: Love (intimate) relationships

Sample issues: Healthy partnering, connection, communication, mutual understanding, appreciation, giving and receiving, affirming and being affirmed, allowing, forgiveness, trustworthy interactions, dating, sexuality, romance, and relationship status—married, divorced, widowed, single.

___ Realm 2: Family relationships

Sample issues: family unit, extended family, adjusting, children and stepchildren, related parenting issues, sibling issues, parents and aging, relationships and nurturing, and end of life and related issues—medical, death, memorial services, estates.

___ Realm 3: Friends and community life

Sample issues: time with friends, belonging, community participation, religious or spiritual organizations, volunteering, socializing, clubs and local groups, and contributing.

___ **Realm 4: Work life, career and finances**

Sample issues: fulfillment and growth in career direction, business interests and entrepreneurship, financial capacity and literacy for now and the future, debt, under-earning, and negotiation skills.

___ **Realm 5: Listening and communicating**

Sample issues: having open and clear communication, creating agreements, freedom to voice what's important, compassion in listening, giving others room to be themselves, honoring each other.

___ **Realm 6: Health and well-being**

Sample issues: your body and aging, health, energy and vitality, strength, exercise and movement, mindfulness, nutrition and hydration, emotional state, re-charging practices, confidence, nutrition choices and habits.

___ **Realm 7: Femininity**

Sample issues: beauty, self-expression, fashion and personal style, sensuality, skin/hair/appearance, and self-care in general.

___ **Realm 8: Your home and physical environment**

Sample issues: your physical space and its design/décor, location, its flow, organization, and level of clutter.

___ Realm 9: Creativity, curiosity, and passions

Sample issues: having fun, creative expression, learning and discovery, hobbies, interests and passions, new directions.

___ Realm 10: Mindset

Sample issues: gratitude, confidence, optimism, adaptability, flexibility, visioning, taking new approaches, shifting viewpoints, and flow.

___ Realm 11: Spirituality and reflection, internal life (being grounded/connected to source)

Sample issues: soul work, expanded heart and practices, inner work practices (meditation, prayer, mantras), boundaries, and working with and through feelings and emotions in ways that serve you.

Once you rank your top three realms on which to focus to navigate joy, think about your challenges that you want to shift. Use what I've suggested or add your own. After all, this is about you and your joy. As with your realms, select two challenges on which you want to focus. Remember, you can always circle back to address other issues later.

Example one: Your realm is love, and intimacy is a priority. Your challenge is that your dating life is not bringing you great prospects. That's a great start. Example two: Your realm is family life, and your issue is that you are butting heads with your children. Example three: Your realm is home, and your issue is that you are drowning in clutter and struggle with getting organized.

Now, write the three realms you want to explore and the leading two challenges in each one that you want to take on that need some sprinkling of joy!

REALM: _____
        Challenge 1: _____
        Challenge 2: _____

REALM: _____
        Challenge 1: _____
        Challenge 2: _____

REALM: _____
        Challenge 1: _____
        Challenge 2: _____

Adding Measurement

Before we work through the five steps of the Joy Activation Process (Awaken-Acknowledge-Act-Adapt Affirm), I'd love for you to consider your current state and the amount of joy in your life at the present time.

1. You know how to let go of the things that don't elevate your life or serve you.

1....2 ....3....4....5....6....7....8....9....10
<I hold onto everything   I'm free!>

2. You're not highly critical of yourself or others. You positively impact people.

1....2 ....3....4....5....6....7....8....9....10
<I criticize everyone.   I look for ways to build others up>

3. You take care of yourself (mind, body, heart, soul).

1....2 ....3....4....5....6....7....8....9....10
<I do nothing for myself   Self-care   is   a   definite priority!>

4. You're comfortable with who you are.

1....2 ....3....4....5....6....7....8....9....10
<Not even close   Overflowing>

5. You know your value.

1....2 ....3....4....5....6....7....8....9....10
<Hideous   Gorgeous>

6. You claim responsibility for your life.

1....2 ....3....4....5....6....7....8....9....10
<Nothing is my fault   I own it!>

7. You are a contributor and bring joy with you wherever you go. .

1....2 ....3....4....5....6....7....8....9....10
<I am miserable   I'm full of joy!>

8. You create your own happiness and you do work that fulfills you.

1....2 ....3....4....5....6....7....8....9....10
<What's happiness?   I jump out of
bed each morning>

9. You are courageously yourself and live fully.

1....2 ....3....4....5....6....7....8....9....10
<Total Scaredy-Cat   I'm my own Superhero!>

10. The only approval you need is your own.

1....2 ....3....4....5....6....7....8....9....10
<I rely on others'   I approve of me>
opinions

11. You forgive yourself and others quickly.

1....2 ....3....4....5....6....7....8....9....10
<*I'm a grudge holder   I'm very forgiving*>

12. You have healthy boundaries.

1....2 ....3....4....5....6....7....8....9....10
<*Others walk all over me.   I'm definite
about what is
acceptable and
communicate that.*>

13. You lead your life from intention, not from competition.

1....2 ....3....4....5....6....7....8....9....10
<*I will win no matter   Intention fuels me*>

14. If something doesn't work, you shift it, not suffer it!

1....2 ....3....4....5....6....7....8....9....10
<*I'm suffering   I'm happy beyond words*>

Where did you find yourself on the continuum as you measured? Most likely, you're toward one end or the other, depending on the statement. If you are at the top end of the continuum, then pick new realms and challenges, so you have something to up-level. Make it worth the work!

If you landed in the middle on many, you might have a slight sense of blah. Maybe you find yourself consistently scoring on the low end across the board and feel some hopelessness. Don't despair.

Maybe no one has ever asked you to rate yourself so honestly before. Remember: You can move the needle on things that you measure! It makes a big difference to understand where you are now, so you can unfold new steps to take and mindsets to shift that will move that scale toward those 10s.

That's what you'll accomplish as you dive into the Joy Activation Process.

Plotting Your Course to Joy

- No matter how hard it may seem, you need honest assessment now to move in the direction you want to go.
- Think of yourself as the tree. The realms are your branches and the challenges are the leaves.
- You need to be ready and willing to shift, and you need to trust yourself in the process.
- Prioritize what to work on first. If you work on too much at once, you'll lack focus to get results. You can always circle back.
- Measure, assess, take new steps, and see how you can move that needle!

Listen to what Maryl has to say about navigating joy at:
gpstojoybook.com

Part 3: Set to Soar

"The hardest prison to escape is in your mind." ~ *Unknown*

At this point, you've learned that you must first be grounded in order to begin to navigate joy. You must accept and actually be grateful for having lost your true north because charting a new course toward wonderful new horizons can only start with being lost and accepting that fact.

We've covered what you need in order to plot your new coordinates in filling your joy tank... and keeping it full. Now you also have a better understanding of navigating your finances and how that skill helps clear your path.

Now it's time to soar, and in this section, I will guide you to find your new direction and the new stars by which you can navigate a joyful life. As your course correction coach, I want to help you gain a celestial view of everything that brings joy into your life. It's time for you to become unlost and find the new trajectory to your joy.

Yes, it takes courage to course correct but the only other choice is to remain stalled... and stay stuck in a joyless existence. I am certain that you don't want that for your life. You have it within you to choose your new reference points and context.

In the last part of this book, I will help you reprogram your own G.P.S. to Joy so that you can find and embrace your own new territories. We'll walk through the Joy

Activation Process together, and you'll learn to chart new paths and how to stay on track once you create them.

I assure you that joy's horizons are profoundly wide, and the higher we go, the further we can see. The deeper we look, the further we can go.

It's time to soar!

Chapter Eight:

The Joy Activation Process

"The key to attention rests in the here and now. Because in the present moment, everything is fresh, rich, larger than life, and most important—actionable." ~ davidji, Sacred Powers

Joy has layers and dimension. In the dimension of joy, the experience of joy can suddenly pop for us, like stars that are born inside the dark matter of our universe. In that space lies the potential for a rich and elevated human experience. When we're children, joy is easy, and we love to naturally discover everything! We are fearless.

When challenging situations happen, joy and happiness become harder. They are reality check moments and they throw a mean punch! We react, feeling some kind of pain or disappointment, and get knocked down. Our joy takes a beating from that loss of innocence. Then we begin to fill the space where joy and love have been with ways to protect ourselves and ward off further unwelcome surprises.

Sometimes, we stop trusting life and for many of us, trust gets replaced with emotional armor and a full arsenal of protective measures to ensure that we survive. In that process, we forget how joy, happiness, and love feel and how to bring them back.

Like Oxygen

Joy is as critical to living as oxygen. We have the option of turning to our metaphoric joy oxygen-tank to feel alive again and keep our natural connection to joy intact. But mostly we contract—actually breathing and moving less and becoming less conscious even though the "oxygen" and space of joy remain constant.

This turns into our new "normal," living from defense and fending off danger, which puts more space between us and joy's source. Why? We cannot be simultaneously on high alert defense mode and also be connected to joy. The two don't mix. You cannot soar when you are contracted.

In short, we trade joy and love for avoiding danger. We get more automated and regulated, filling ourselves up with standard pursuits of work and family, financial gain, community involvement—all the stuff of living. But what we don't do is shift ourselves back to thriving by reconnecting to joy.

> *You have to spread your wings to soar. You won't get off the ground when you are contracted.*

We get so accustomed to the routine that we forget what the lightness of joy even feels like and then come to believe that this way of living—numb and disconnected—is normal.

We've all been there, submerged in dark reactions to life's toughest transitions. We lose our way back to joy where light lives.

We have a constant internal "battle" in which we are either getting by, giving up, or fighting like hell to defend what's ours. We get what we can, like everything is a limited resource. We grasp for any relief we can find even if that brings us harm. But the harder we grasp for joy or love or happiness, the more we realize we can't secure it... **because joy, happiness and love are intangible.** You can't hold and have them! They are a space that we make room for when we shift mindsets, act from love, and change up our points of view.

Making Space for Joy through the Joy Activation Process

College football is a fierce game of transitions that is about so much more than the score. With each play, the players execute strategy knowing there are an infinite number of factors that can't be controlled.

You could say that we play a similar game. Without having sufficient information to be comfortable, we tackle daily challenges to move down the field we call our lives.

Our opponents are internal. They go by many names — fear, negative thinking, being hard on ourselves, compulsive habits, imposing expectations, trying to control what we can't, and more. These opponents initially can unravel us, upend our efforts, and have us laser-focused on our failures. As we refine how to tackle them, we quickly adapt to outcomes and create new approaches more rapidly.

Yes, we get thrown off balance and stopped. For a bit. But the deeper game is that we grow wiser in how we play and that we keep playing. With each fumble and failed execution, we learn. We gain wisdom as we go for yards. Some plays are so life-altering that they steal our joy, tear at our trust, and stop us, causing us to question ourselves, our lives, and everyone in it. Our confidence is challenged as our capacities are further tested.

There comes a time as you play against your opponent when you are tired of feeling held back by them without an action plan to confront them. You are no longer all right with staying stagnant, feeling derailed, being without joy, and not knowing what to do next. The Joy Activation Process is designed to navigate your joy and connect you to your dreams, getting you out of stagnation, moving down that field, and playing again!

No Playbook & Doing it Anyway

I've shared with you that I discovered the Joy Activation Process when tough personal losses upended my life, especially my husband's cancer that turned me into a young widow. When I promised David before he died that I would live the best life I could, I quickly realized that I had no playbook for that! From that promise, the Joy Activation Process emerged and fueled my growth, choice by choice, new action by new action, and softened the intense impact of grief and fear.

> *No matter how difficult, transitions will always be part of navigating your joy.*

We all face transitions! In the last year, I've guided many people (the majority being women) through the Joy Activation Process. With it, they have reinvented aspects of their lives to find joy again. They have connected to what they want and need after these transitions with truth and clarity. They have found their new true norths.

Three Stories

To illustrate how to approach the Joy Activation Process, I share stories of three women who I've guided through the process. As they applied it, they got clarity, they chose specific new actions, and achieved new outcomes. Going through the process shed light on their specific situations, helped them articulate what they desired, and gave them a path to connect with joy through new choices and new actions.

Meet Sarah. The death of her child was the hardest thing she'd ever experienced. Being the primary caregiver left Sarah so spent, she had no idea how to move forward. She'd been caregiving full-time during her daughter's illness, which lasted for many years. Her health suffered as did her marriage. She and her husband had no time for each other because they were hyper-focused on their daughter. They had given so much that they were exhausted and filled with grief. Sarah came to me grieving, wanting to discover what could be next for her, and how to bring life back to her marriage. She really just wanted to stop everything but knew that was the grief talking, not her true self. She used the Joy Activation Process to bring form to what she now wanted. She was able to move herself forward. One of her first actions was to select a grief counselor for her husband and herself. That initial step helped pave the way for working through the grief together and reuniting.

Another woman, Melissa, loved her work as a hospital physical therapist, but she did not love the demanding schedule. As it was, she had little time for herself and no time for her friends who complained that she was always M.I.A. for their get-togethers. Her family was chronically upset by her late hours and accompanying stress level. She would arrive home tightly wound and short tempered. Her kids were athletes and they missed her involvement. Previously, she had been very involved with their teams and training. Her husband loved her and missed the Melissa he knew! He wanted his wife back. Contributing financially was important to her, but over time, the cost to her joy and happiness was too much.

I guided her to use the Joy Activation Process. She saw new actions she wanted to take, and she made them based on what she dreamed of for herself and her family. Over time, step by step, choice by choice, action by action, she constructed her work life so her financial contribution was sufficient, her stress levels reduced; she had more time for her own health, and she configured her schedule so she could be with her family. They absolutely saw and felt the difference!

I also worked with Diane who was at a crossroads in her career, in her marriage, and with her finances. She'd felt zero spark with her husband *and* was bored with her job even though she really liked her co-workers and company. She also knew very little about their finances, but she was aware that they were not on track to financial stability. At first, her way to deal with her unhappiness included too many happy hours. She turned her back on caring for herself or her finances. It got to a point at which it hurt too much. With the Joy Activation Process, she was willing to actually envision what she wanted for her work, in her marriage, and with her finances. She wanted to work in a different department, wanted to talk with her husband again, and needed to deal with her credit card debt and living expenses now. She was tired of feeling so tired, drained, and resigned over all of it. She put the process to work!

Sarah, Melissa, and Diane each used the Joy Activation Process to elevate their lives. They took the time to pause, break things down, reflect, and reinvent as they faced their most pressing challenges. From discovering new purpose, to taking on their health and energy, finding a new work direction, and modifying the quality of their marriages, they put the process to the test.

The power of the Joy Activation Process is that it's a tool to use after even the toughest transitions that guides you to new choices and new actions that are truer, more fulfilling, and stem from a place of joy and creativity.

Steps in the Joy Activation Process

The steps in the Joy Activation Process include:
- Awaken
- Acknowledge
- Act
- Adapt
- Affirm

The Joy Activation Process is best applied to your most urgent challenges, so you can uncover and tackle the obstacles that block the outcomes you want.

A tip before you get started: consider what you could release that is no longer serving you. It makes a big difference because whatever is stumping you—mindsets, attitudes, ideas, thoughts, or beliefs—releasing them makes way for new actions. I call this surrendering to the goodbyes.

As we've covered, you must accept being lost in order to chart a new course.

Embracing the power of surrendering to the goodbyes brings to light new choices and actions. As you unfold your dreams and desires, what there is to release becomes clearer.

I recommend that you take a stab at assessing what is between you and your dreams. My dreams get hindered by expectations and unresolved emotional ties. Pull the hood up on them to let them out. Then it's much easier to reinvent.

> **Trust the process.**
>
> **Take the step.**

We can use transitions to redirect. Weathering them expands us and accelerates our capacity to make choices in the face of being lost. Facing them lets us replace being totally stopped by fear with trusting the process. New coordinates arise and come into view and that gives our lives renewed energy.

It's amazing to watch new paths emerge! The transitions can put us in a tumble where we have no control. But that's not entirely true. We still control our mindset, our choices, and our new actions. The Joy Activation Process has us harness those three things. The Process begins with one challenge to address and asks that we honestly say what we want that would deal with it. That starts with dreaming, imagining, seeing it in our mind's eye.

Together, we will move through the steps using Sarah's, Diane's, and Melissa's situations as real-life examples of the process in action! (Note: Their answers to the various questions in each exercise appear in italicized type.)

Awaken

To awaken, we take stock of <u>where we are now so we</u> <u>have a starting point.</u>

To recap Sarah's story: She was dealing with extreme fatigue, the death of her child, finding a new path for her health and her life, and putting life back into her marriage. Sarah wanted to find reasons to keep going. She wanted to discover herself as she is now and where to go from there. She mostly wanted to reconnect with her husband.

Sarah's Main Challenge:

I'm exhausted and have no energy, I'm sadder than I've ever been, and I don't even know where to start.

Step 1: Awaken:

What SPECIFICALLY do you want instead?

I WANT: *To know how my body is doing; I want to find a reason to go on and to have energy again. It's been too long since I laughed with my husband, and I want to touch him again. I want to find a new direction in my work that has me feeling relevant and that I truly enjoy.*

Dreaming now, what would you consider a better outcome?

That I actually want to eat! I am moving again to regain my strength. I have the will to carry on and maybe even feel less sad and worried all the time, and my husband and I find our way through this together. I find a part-time job close to my house.

What is missing for you that if you added it would provide more harmony for you?

Time to rest. Friends. A good cry. Long hugs from my husband. The will to go on.

For something new to emerge, what would you need to say goodbye to right now?

Guilt that we could have done more for our daughter; my daughter being my entire focus; that I have to sacrifice everything and all of me, even my health, to make it through the day; and that there's a right way to grieve and a time when it ends.

What takes your joy out when you think of this challenge that you would be willing to address?

What takes my joy out is the agonizing feeling like we could have done more for our daughter and feeling so depleted over my husband and me losing our connection. I worry about whether our marriage will survive.

Why shift it? What benefit would be worth facing this challenge? What's important enough to you that you'd be willing to adjust for it without knowing exactly what comes next?

Feeling alive again like I don't want to die, being in love again with my husband, getting my strength back so I can enjoy life again.

Acknowledge

Acknowledging where you are in the moment is the next step in the Joy Activation Process. To better understand this step, I will share Melissa's answers. Melissa is the hospital physical therapist who had a conflict between the love for her work and demands of her schedule, and the impact of this on her family and health.

Step 2: Acknowledge

What's the impact on your life from the challenge right now? Are you suffering anything about it?

I'm totally conflicted. I love what I do and the people who I help. My income is vital to the family. I love my family more than anything and get so stressed that I take it out on them. Doing a good job as a mother, wife, and therapist is very important to me. My husband loves me so much and supports me, but I can see how sad and sullen he gets when I'm always so stressed and short with him.

I AM SUFFERING.

I'm suffering because I love my family and want to be involved like I was before, but I constantly worry about our finances even though I know we are financially good. I know it's not a rational fear.

I don't take care of myself and am worried that I could get injured if I don't get serious about exercising properly.

ARE YOU BEING HARD ON YOURSELF ABOUT IT?

I am being hard on myself because I want to do it all perfectly. I love everybody so much. I just can't keep up. I'm strong, but I run out of steam as life gets more complex. Something has to give, but I feel badly because I love my work, my patients and my family, yet I don't want my husband to feel dumped on.

Is there something about this issue that you just don't want to deal with? Is there an expectation you have that's not being met?

I am avoiding having a conversation with my husband about what I'm struggling with and about our finances to see what other ways I could structure my time and work. I'm afraid we will get into a fight or not find a solution. We have money put aside, and I think I could work part time. But I keep pushing myself. I'm not sure why I do that.

I DO HAVE AN UNMET EXPECTATION WHICH IS:

I can see that I definitely feel like I'm falling short. I'm not meeting my own expectations of myself. I should be able to do it all, right? I feel like I'm failing everybody – myself, my work, my family, my husband, even my friends. I hate this feeling!

Act: NOW Actions versus NEW Actions

Only after you have awakened to and acknowledged the specific challenge and the impact on your life can you begin shifting, and I call that shift "now actions versus new actions."

Diane was the woman at the crossroads of her career and her marriage. She wanted to find a new direction at work and was not even sure she wanted to stay married. Her ignorance about the family finances had her paralyzed with fear to do anything new. She saw no solution but to "deal with it." She was so unhappy that she was finally open to see what else she could do besides live with it. Through the first two steps in the process—awakening and acknowledging, Diane envisioned what she wanted for both her career and marriage, including where she might want to live if she separated, the kind of relationship she wanted with her husband if she didn't, and the type of work that would inspire her while providing the income that she needed to be in charge of her own finances.

Step 3: Act—NOW Actions vs. NEW Actions

NOW: What actions are you taking now?

1. Staying in a job I don't like for the health benefits and because it's safe and easy.

2. Going to happy hour after work with friends and colleagues, getting home late a few nights a week.

3. Living separately from my husband in the second bedroom. We don't spend time together because he works so much, and we don't coordinate our schedules to be together.

What do you see about how your *NOW* actions are causing you to suffer on this?

I have not looked at any other work options or even talked to the company about working in another department. My husband and I do nothing together right now. He travels a lot for work and I stopped caring. We don't work at our relationship. We both live separate lives but don't address it. I haven't talked to him about what he wants now or shared with him what I want now because I haven't even thought much about it.

NEW: What *NEW* actions could you take now to have a shift?

Now Action	Keep/Replace?	NEW Action
Keep job as is	*Keep job & possibly replace*	*Talk to HR about other opportunities*

Going out to avoid going home	*Replace*	*Replace happy hour with exercise; invite husband out; make easy conversation with him*
Not talking to him truthfully	*Replace*	*Talking to him with a 3rd party to talk about what we both want now, admitting mutual apathy*

Adapt

There is more than adjusting your actions. You also will want to define a plan and allow time for that plan to work on the challenge to get what you want instead.

Let's return to Melissa and her issue of her demanding schedule in the job she loves.

Step 4: Adapt to new actions

Anchor new actions by giving them three to four weeks to make an impact on your issue. WRITE YOUR SPECIFIC NEW ACTION(S) AND THE TIME FRAME YOU ARE ALLOWING YOURSELF TO ABSORB THOSE ACTIONS:

1. After speaking with her husband about finances and to the hospital about her work schedule, Melissa is taking one month to work part time, and she and her husband are now looking at the difference the lower income will make and what they can do to adjust family expenses, so she can be home more. They've already calculated this prior to taking the part-time job but will take a second look, so they keep track and have financial peace of mind.

2. Melissa has called her friends and has proposed a monthly happy hour meet-up. She also told them about her new work situation. Her friends are putting her in touch with other part-time gigs they know about, so she can keep her options open for work in case the hospital can't sustain the current work plan. She is also looking at employment options closer to home.

3. Melissa is plugging back in with her kids' teams to see how she can support them, and she and her husband have reinstated date night.

Also, as part of the Adapt step, I'd like you to read over the 14 habits to navigating your joy. Feel free to circle up to three that would make a difference in your ability to face the challenge. The habits bring fuel to the process and are listed below. I've placed an asterisk by the three that Sarah chose to fuel her life. .

1. You let go of the things that no longer serve to support and elevate you.
2. You're not highly critical of yourself or others.
3. **You have routines to take care of your mind, body, heart, and soul.***
4. You're comfortable with yourself.
5. You know your value.
6. You claim responsibility for your life.
7. You contribute and bring joy to people.
8. **You create your own happiness and you do work that fulfills you.***
9. You have the courage to be yourself and live fully.
10. The only approval you seek now is your own.

11. *You forgive yourself and others quickly. You are not a grudge holder.**
12. You have healthy boundaries.
13. You lead your life from intention, not competition.
14. If something is not working, you shift it. You don't spend time steeped suffering!

Developing a personal motto is also part of the Adapt step of the Joy Activation Process. When I had her write one, Sarah wrote this:

I am grateful for the love I have and how committed I am to all that I do. I know everyone is always learning. I forgive myself and others quickly, and I trust my choices, knowing my well-intentioned actions will keep me on a great track.

Affirm

The last step in the process involves affirming the new actions you have taken to improve outcomes on the challenge(s) you are facing. It's so rich and important to affirm ourselves and our actions as part of celebrating ourselves and our results. The joy this brings is palpable!

Please take a look at how you scored on the Joy Scale before using the process and notice if you now see where some measures have moved up. I suspect you'll also feel more connected to the 14 power habits!

Here's how the affirmation step looks in Diane's situation:

1. Check in and affirm that the NEW ACTIONS are giving you a better outcome on the issue:

Diane has spoken to HR about other opportunities. Other options require training, so she is thinking about whether or not she's willing to do that. She has also started to walk after work and asked her husband to join her on the weekends. He's agreed to go for walks. She will begin to dialog with her husband again for the next month, so they can set a foundation to address their more vulnerable issues with the help of a counselor.

2. In what realms is life really working? Own it here! List one to three realms in which life is working well:

Realm of Work: *Diane has a job.*

Realm of Community: *Diane has friends she spends time with.*

Realm of Home: *She and her husband have a home and are not discussing divorce or separation.*

Next, write down up to three circumstances that are right where you want them:

Diane enjoys her friends, likes her neighborhood, and enjoys her colleagues.

3. Affirm yourself for being in action. Read the following statement and add your own affirmation(s) to it:

"I am regularly taking actions to face my challenges and am willing to keep on learning and growing and living my life from my dreams and what I desire, **ONE CHOICE AT A TIME.**"

Diane's affirmation: *I am choosing my own path forward and understand that my NEW actions are taking me in my new direction."*

My Own Joy Activation Process

My relationship with my adult daughter is evolving. Here is how I used the process to create our relationship and to continue to grow.

Maryl's Realm: *Family*

Background: *My daughter is a recent college graduate who attended university out-of-state. With that, I've been in empty-nest mode and am accustomed to living solo. She moved back home after working overseas for six months.*

What doesn't work? *We can butt heads easily. I don't like having my home disrupted with messes I didn't make, discovering stains on the couch from a spilled drink, and finding an empty toilet paper supply at the most critical of moments. I don't react well when she gets afraid and lets her emotions fly. Then friction between us ensues, especially when she refuses to discuss a topic that I consider important.*

She depends on me in many ways for love, for my strength and my patience, to be there while she gets on her feet financially, and to be a judgment-free parent so she can try new things, fail and try again. She is in the transition from college graduate to new in the work force. I am searching for how to best support her now as she finds her new footing. I don't want her to panic as I set new boundaries for what I will do and stop doing now. Is it my role to push her? To stand back and let her unfold her future on her own? What does support look like now? Now what is my role?

Maryl's Challenge: *There is no guide book for "adulting" and transitioning my daughter from older teenager to young woman. She's in between new pursuits. Sometimes, she seems 30 and other times, 16. She's my only child. I have no previous parenting experience to fall back on. Embarking on new things can*

106

trigger anxiety and I can get uptight pretty easily. That's because I have this automatic thought that I need to get it right or something could go really wrong. I'm as ready to move on with my own life as she is. We both are in a major transition.

1. Awaken

What specifically do I want instead? *I want us to have great communication and stay connected where we really hear each other. No fireworks needed. I want to support her to believe in herself, grow her confidence, and do what fulfills her. We both love and support each other through our own transitions.*

If I honestly look, what would be a better outcome?
Me letting go of being her fixer and letting her be.

That she and I both lighten up through this time in our lives and choose pursuits that flow from our dreams and visions — from whom we love, to the work that calls us, and everything in between. That we are loving with each other, especially during the tough moments. That we both embrace that life is inherently perfect, especially the challenging parts.

What is missing for me that, if added, would provide more harmony for me?

1. Getting clear for myself what sort of support I am comfortable providing to her during this transition.

2. Updating the boundaries. Having a new agreement between us that provides mutual respect of what we both need in our lives at this stage.

2. Doing something to quiet my mind each morning, like yoga or meditation or writing.

3. Letting go where, candidly, I would prefer to control her future. Instead, focusing on my own choices and being direct with her about what I need and how I want us to interact now.

5. Stop worrying and feeling guilty about anything from the past and making peace that there will probably always be growing pains for both of us.

What would I need to say goodbye to right now so that something new can emerge?

1. That there is a right way to approach this and that there is anything wrong.

2. Controlling, manipulating, and feeling like there's any parenting failure I need to compensate for.

3. Fear of losing our connection especially if either of us gets upset.

4. That grappling or failing is a bad thing or avoidable.

5. Treating her like she's a fragile, incapable child.

2. Acknowledge

The impact of our issue is I'm annoyed and feel out of sorts when we are butting heads. I shut down and want to send her to attitude boot camp because I know I'm right. What I want instead? For us to talk through whatever comes up as it comes up so we can move through it and move on.

3. Actions — NOW versus NEW

NOW: Going it alone. Getting shut down when she gets emotional then getting resentful myself. Feeling frustrated and stuck because I don't know how to manage this.

NEW: Trust that we will get through anything together and that if either of us gets upset, we both have the ability to deal with it. Getting support from people who have gone through this transition already. I could also find someone to work through my side of the transition equation and learn some new communication approaches that get the result I want while keeping our bond loving and strong.

4. Adapt

I am gaining a better understanding about what's important to her and what she needs in our relationship. She's getting to know me better, too. We have girl time dates together, like getting our nails done, cooking dinner as often as we can, or having some Sunday afternoon beach time. We are finding new ways to work through daily life logistics like grocery shopping, house chores, financial matters, and more. We are slowly adjusting to living under the same roof again after so many years of living apart. At the same time, she's getting clear on what's involved for her to live on her own now that she's moved back. I check how I communicate with her so our conversations are productive and kind. When I'm feeling righteous about anything, I let that go, take a cleansing breath, and simply have a conversation with her. Neither of us wants drama, so when it starts to brew between us, we interrupt that as best we can and find our way to options we both can live with.

5. Affirm

My new actions are building a deeper bond between us where our mutual love and respect is beyond question. Our talks are great most of the time and there is much less antagonism. We both have our unique focus on what we want to develop in ourselves. We support that in each other as we balance our interdependence with our individual personalities.

I have included a worksheet with the Joy Activation Process in the Resource section at the end of this book. Please put it to work! Initially, you'll complete only the first three steps (Awaken, Acknowledge, and Act). You will then need time to Adapt the **new** actions you select for yourself. Finally, you will work on the Affirm step and go back to that step as needed.

Plotting Your Course to Joy

- Joy is as abundant as oxygen! We need to find our way to taking more in.
- Step 1: Awaken—define and clarify where you are and what is happening now, and articulate what you desire for your life instead.
- Step 2: Acknowledge—be honest about the impact your challenge is having on your life and what you're tolerating around this challenge.

- Step 3: Act—list out your NOW actions that are keeping you stuck and identify what NEW actions you can take that will bring joy back into your life.
- Step 4: Adapt—give yourself a few weeks to adapt to your plan and allow it to take hold to generate the outcomes you desire. Create a personal motto.
- Step 5: Affirm—affirm that the outcomes you want are taking shape from your new actions and that more joy is coming back into your life as you upgrade.

Listen to what Maryl has to say about navigating joy at:
gpstojoybook.com

Chapter Nine:

Joy's Reference Points

"Let go of your attachment to being right, and suddenly your mind is more open. You're able to benefit from the unique viewpoints of others without being crippled by your own judgment." ~ Ralph Marston

Now that you more fully understand the steps in the Joy Activation Process — Awakening, Acknowledging, Acting, Adapting, and Affirming — it's time to cover the reference points you can use to keep yourself on a joyful course. I'll outline the reference points or "bedrocks of joy" that provide a foundation and context for joy to emerge. These, in a nutshell, are my fundamental values — the coordinates of my G.P.S. to Joy — and work hand-in-hand with the Joy Activation Process. When I honor my values, I experience joy.

Trust the Transitions

As I took a closer look at the barrage of transitions and losses I faced in almost one sitting, I had an Aha! moment. I saw that life is inherently perfect in ways I don't need to understand. I saw that life is a continuous flow of transitions that range from minor to life-altering. This was very humbling, as I came to see that we simply cannot control life's transitions. However, how we see the impact of these transitions is really a matter of personal perspective.

One person's easy speed bump is another person's Armageddon, right? Take a moment and think: What are your biggest transitions so far? Have you experienced divorce or betrayal, lost a loved one, had a major career change, gone through turmoil financially or dealt with a health crisis?

Whether minor or life-altering, please trust the transitions. They make up our lives! You've heard the expression, "Nothing remains the same, except change." Resisting change cultivates misery, leaving joy by the wayside.

Be Willing Not to Know

Beyond trusting the transitions, we also need to strengthen our ability to make peace with not knowing the exact nature or timing of our outcomes. This is what I call the "in-between," and I realize it is uncomfortable, especially when prolonged. However, when we honor the "in-between," our connection to joy stops depending on outcomes unfolding in any particular way.

> *Every transition opens a new path. Allow yourself to go with the flow!*

Even with that muscle built, joy still needs us to move beyond where we are and go to places we've never been. We could just call it "going with the flow." Each transition opens up a new path, and looking down that path at first glance, we often don't see where it leads. At that defining moment, our compass becomes the courage and trust to step onto the path, regardless of how obscured the path might look, and to move forward into joy.

114

When we resist taking that step, we block joy and force ourselves back into the dark recesses of our fears and anxieties. Simply resisting can take more from us than facing the thing we are trying to avoid! I know because I have to deal with myself on this regularly. It can be a major source of suffering. When we release ourselves from needing to know, we relax and stop demanding the relief of immediate answers. Then we invite in new ways of seeing and experiencing our lives—which is its own form of joy!

Personally, I replace my addiction to "knowing" everything with a delicious daily cup of hot chocolate at my favorite local coffee haunt. Chocolate brings me joy. Stressing because I must know does not.

Get Your Expectations into the Open

Silent suffering…. It's a habit that stomps on joy. Yet, it's a common condition that looks like a fundamental belief that others' needs come first, often to the exclusion of our own. Its source could be cultural, biological or familial. No matter; this belief has many of us feeling disconnected and emotionally estranged from ourselves.

I stand by another belief: We all merit being valued, and that begins with valuing ourselves. That implies that everyone's needs have equal importance. Voicing our own needs and expectations honors our value and others' value. When we speak rather than stay silent, we often come back to joy because it's really challenging for joy and silent suffering to co-exist!

I'm not suggesting that you make meaningless demands of others for sport. I simply see the value in giving voice to your needs and expectations. Do it lovingly, with yourself first, then with your mate, your partner, children, family, friends, co-workers, etc. People generally can't read your mind. When you communicate clearly what you need, want, and expect with the people around you, new paths and amazing intersections form that make way for the joy of connection.

Take Self-Discovery to New Heights

By trusting the transitions and opening yourself up to new paths and perspectives, you're practicing greater self-awareness. You begin your journey as you embrace and discover what activates joy within you.

I value learning and partake in daily practices to grow and improve in my life. The Joy Activation Process is constructed as a learning tool that can be used any time as a means to discover and grow. This practice will continue having you take your self-discovery to new heights and likely ignite joy beyond what you imagined.

> *Communication allows you to more effectively navigate joy.*

Grow, my friend. Grow from your dreams! Activate your joy. Up-level your life. Get set to soar!

Courageously Claim Your Choices

Beyond sharing your expectations with others, claim your choices courageously and with conviction. They are your choices and they give you the actions that will have your dreams come to life. It might seem that not all your choices and correlative actions are direct routes to your dreams realized. That's okay. Many choices and actions are also stepping stones.

Ultimately, the act of staying connected to your vision and dreams will guide you toward a new outcome that needs to emerge. Tune into your power to make your own choice and trust the process!

My inner work has allowed me to build up huge capacities to experience joy. I also understand more about what drives my personal choices, which helps me steer away from repeating choices that definitely do not bring joy. I value learning from the contrast, too!

A final note: check to see where you might allow others to dictate choices for you that conflict with your values and course correct that for yourself. Only you can keep yourself on your own track.

Turn Your Joy Ignition on Everyday

Here are some ways to create joy in your life. With each, I provide an affirmation at the beginning.

I value taking decisive action daily from joy. This is both an intention and mindset. Daily, I create joy through self-care, service to others, music and dancing, and learning something new every day. Get curious about the daily actions you can enjoy. Turn your joy ignition on!

Act from Love

"Ride love's horse, and think nothing of the journey – for love's horse knows the way quite well ... in one charge, with one movement it delivers you to the next station—even if the road is not smooth." ~ Rumi

I value acting from love. To begin, I ask you to take a deeper cut at discerning your personal need to take better  care of yourself while learning about others' needs more deeply, too. By sharing your mutual expectations and needs, you refine how to act from love with each other.

Joy flourishes when we come from love. Taking actions from love creates micro-shifts in the most challenging issues, which lead to even bigger shifts. Acting from love leads to outcomes I want, often with the added bonus of other amazing outcomes I had no way to predict!

Speak your love. Boldly tell others how much you love and appreciate them. It is a fulfilling practice and has a huge impact on joy — yours and theirs!

I value love with gratitude. Whenever I take action from love and gratitude, I find life has a sweet flow.

Connect

I deeply value connection and hold my relationships as gold. Joy thrives from connection and interconnection with our closest relationships and in our communities. Part of that equation is also the connection we have to our commitments and intentions. When we do what we say we will do, we foster deeper connections and profound trust.

Joy also lives inside our interconnectedness — we are there for others and they for us. It sounds simple, but many of us struggle with receiving and prefer to give.

I value the energy exchange of give and take. I see how everyone is elevated by that dynamic. We need each other on so many levels. This is why connection is such a vital part of joy.

Be Curious and Play

Remember playing in the sandbox? Imagine doing that now! Just for a minute or do it for a day! Watch how your joy levels rise and how alive you feel. There's a joyful magic when we lighten up and stop taking ourselves so seriously.

The best masks come off with our besties!

Laugh. Let go and let yourself be.

When I do that, every day is another chance to play. Because I'm naturally curious, I see and learn new things and even the simplest things become wondrous. I delight in a child's laughter, the beauty of a flower, the sound of the waves, and watching the wind blow through the ficus tree in my garden. When we soften, our experience of joy heightens. With practice, you can ignite your joy just by raising your "curiosity" bar and finding more ways to play.

Let Go of Being Right

Tough one, I know. I struggle with this one myself. But joy needs us to tame this tiger!

> *The need to be right and joy can simply not co-exist. Opt for joy!*

When we get fixated on being right, we shut off the love valve. We quickly lose perspective, and the joy that comes from our natural playfulness slips away. For me, my being-right habit can damage my most intimate connections. When you find yourself needing to be right, ask what the outcome will be if you stay rigid. I doubt you'll find much joy there.

We simply cannot be open-minded and right at the same time, and joy cannot exist in a close-minded environment. I find that as I make it a point to let go of being right, my relationships and conversations flow easier and are more uplifting, especially the difficult conversations. NOTE: You can be right and not be righteous about it. Letting go of being right activates my joy. I trust it will have the same effect for you.

"To fly higher, release the excess baggage you don't need anymore."

Plotting Your Course to Joy

- Transitions are necessary. Trust them.
- Accept the unknown and you will be lighter, more joyful.
- Communicate your expectations. No one is a mind-reader.
- Embark on the journey of self-discovery to live true to yourself and activate your joy.
- Make your own choices and own them.
- Take the steps needed to create joy daily.
- Do everything from a position of love.
- Joy needs connectedness to thrive.
- Go out and play!
- Let go of being right.

Listen to what Maryl has to say about navigating joy at:
gpstojoybook.com

Chapter Ten:

Captain Your Communication: Words Matter

You never want to hear the pilot say, "Oh, damn!" Yes, words matter.

"Sticks and stones may break my bones but words will never hurt me," is an old adage crafted to tend to the delicate hearts of children. Words can hurt, and they can also be used to create and reinvent!

Have you noticed how words can either squelch confidence or build it? Or how they can express love or push love away? I noticed how quickly thoughtless comments weaken family connections, crush esteem, cause distrust, and shake up family unity.

I know many of us are no strangers to beating ourselves up with the incessant inner-head chatter only to find ourselves in bed watching too many reruns because our energy has been robbed by our negative self-talk. We've all witnessed words spoken in moments of rage, words so harsh that we become filled with anger in response, or we are overcome with fear and have our confidence and sanity shaken. Hurtful words diminish and even eliminate joy.

Who among us hasn't felt the sting of gossip? I don't know anyone who hasn't felt the humiliation of derision and backstabbing. In this scenario, words kill off confidence, leaving many feeling alone, shamed and unworthy. Just as sad, friendships can become decimated by political rhetoric taken to the extreme, to the point of ending friendships, dividing families and creating giant rifts in communities.

On personal levels and communally, words have the power to change anything and impact any circumstance! Words as tools have the power to win over hearts and minds (starting with our own) on any issue we want to impact. Indeed, the pen is mightier than the sword.

Words give form to what is important to us. They can be spoken as commitments, intentions, vows, promises, prayers, stories, affirmations, mantras, and the like. Whatever their form, words begin the process of inspired actions and unfold the roadmap for what we will create next. I often use words as affirmations to change my point of view or recalibrate my attitude and thinking. Prayers aid me in letting go of what I don't need. Words infused with intention can have us shift our mindsets, giving way to changing how we see and process any situation.

> *Words matter and can be incredibly destructive whether spoken to yourself or someone else.*

When we grasp the potency of words, we can use their power to reinvent, create, and ignite joy! Living from clear commitments attracts joy. The biggest joy stealer? Negative-speak. Spoken out loud or in our heads as self-talk, negative words repel joy.

Words generate our dreams and desires. People who are oriented toward joy understand and harness the power of words to bring their dreams into existence. Powerful outcomes take launch and upgrade our lives.

By the same token, negative-speak—in the form of negative self-talk, expressions of doubt, fear, or distrust—can have the effect of stifling shifts or upgrades we want.

Personal Mantras and Affirmations

Before I learned joy can be ignited by using personal mantras and affirmations, I focused instead on striving for some ideal. I call it the painful pursuit of perfectionism. I was chronically hard on myself and lived in a constant state of anxiousness, like I was not getting life "right."

Before being more active with prayer, mantras, and affirmations, I attempted to mask my failings and to fix my flaws. I hope what I'm about to share with you does *not* sound familiar! If it does, take heart. I'll share a better way to captain your own communications, both with yourself and others.

I felt like I had failed miserably when I became a divorcee who had only one child. I thought, "Now, Helena will be alone without a sibling and it's my fault!" I also suppressed a lot. I spent mounds of energy putting a smile on my face, being graciously measured, even when I was highly annoyed. My mission in life was:

1. To be the perfect single mom, so my daughter wouldn't be so heartbroken by the turbulent custody situation.
2. To get enough sleep, leading me to anxiety pills to stop my chronic worry at night.
3. To eat organic food, with dinner ready every night by 6 p.m.
4. To be filled with energy and good cheer—so strained most nights, I was ready to crash by 8

p.m. — while executing everything just right. Damned exhausting!

After years of chasing crazy expectations of my own design, my joy was drained! Not only could I *not* measure up (who could?), it finally dawned on me I was just punishing myself and running on a spinning "mouse wheel" of feeling like a constant failure. It stirred up shame, self-doubt and second guessing! My compulsive, critical voice drove me to my edge. Talk about joy sucking!

Through life's transitions, that damned inner voice has opinions and judgments on everything. It's main commentary? "You missed the mark *again*!" And, "Don't try it because you'll mess it up!" Draining and confidence killing for sure! To get relief from the effect of that constant chatter, I looked for ways to be kinder to myself. I found ways to be lighter and give that chatter less airtime and power over my actions. I became a better communication captain.

Another thing I did was catch myself in the act of being my harshest critic. I could then lighten up. Being lighter fed my creativity, nourished my heart, had me laughing, helped me heal my love connections, and ignited joy.

> *A personal mantra adjusts your mindset and re-aligns your brain and thoughts.*

I now use words in so many awesome ways! In my writing, poetry, my speaking. I use words as mantras and affirmations to reprogram my brain and actions. I reframe stories about the past and uncover mindsets that stunt my growth.

Understanding the power of words to shrink us, I saw that they can also build us up and give us more personal power than we might have imagined. The personal mantra I created after my husband died is: "No drama, and don't get stuck."

I still recite this to myself when I get side tracked or distracted from actions that move me forward. I repeat it as often as necessary when the chatter in my head starts to override the fight-or-flight reactions. This sort of communication—your own mantra—will help you stay on course and navigate joy.

It's time to consider your own personal mantra and affirmations. If mine resonates with you, use it. Pick a mantra and post it where you'll see it every morning. Read it daily to yourself a few times and recite it when negative self-talk begins to invade your brain! It will start to sink in for you.

Your words have the power to lift you to new heights and out of despair. Let words do their magic!

Here are some suggested personal mantras for you to play with:

- I like who I am.
- I learn from every experience and discover new ways to recharge myself.
- I'm open to changes that serve my life.
- When I struggle, that's my signal that there's something to let go of.
- Let me check in. Am I choosing based on my desired outcomes?
- I know that my failures are exactly what I need to learn and grow.

- Every day is a new opportunity to strengthen a different aspect of myself.
- I'm keeping it positive today.
- I quickly forgive.
- I have the strength to face any challenge in my life.
- I choose love.
- I focus on what I want, not on what I don't want.
- I find peace in making my own choices, whether I succeed or fail.
- What can I do for somebody today?
- I am in the perfect space for my next transition.
- I value the give and take of my life.
- I deeply value connection and hold my relationships as gold.
- I am grounded in gratitude.
- Joy flourishes when I come from love.

The Joy a Vow Can Bring

Can you recall the last time you made a no-turning-back vow?

Maybe it was the first day you walked onto your college campus, completely excited, vowing to complete your degree. Or when you were so filled up that you said, "YES!" to dating exclusively, getting engaged, or even getting married. You may have vowed to commit yourself to that person for a relationship filled with joy and happiness. Then you may have ended it, vowing to honor yourself by leaving. Maybe your vow was a fitness or health promise to yourself, or you simply vowed to enjoy your life and suffer less. Or maybe you made a simple vow to help someone in need.

Clarissa vowed to her daughter, Beth, that she would love her unconditionally and be her rock, that she would look ahead for Beth when life got too cloudy to see a clear path, and that she would be Beth's unwavering supporter through even the messiest of times. Clarissa believed in her daughter, even when she didn't believe in herself.

Beth is now 24, and that vow helped Clarissa work through the emotional ups and downs that come with raising a teen into adulthood. Although there were the inevitable head-buttings over boyfriends, piercings, broken curfew, annoying hooky days, and the like, Clarissa stayed true to her vow. She expanded as a parent by learning how to judge Beth less and focus on bigger picture choices that Beth must make for herself. She adapts her attachment as Beth matures. Not easy! The vow to be Beth's rock and love her unconditionally has given Clarissa deep gratitude for the gift of motherhood and the joyful experience of unconditional love—especially with the pull-your-hair-out moments that raising a child brings!

Clarissa experienced what my friend and horse racing guru, Jimmy the Hat calls a "trifecta of life's transitions." Her sister died, her best friend was diagnosed with cancer, and her husband was injured on the job. After all that, she vowed to reinvent herself in small ways, finding little joys daily and adjusting her mindset to prepare for life as an empty nester as Beth moved out. She became the navigator in caring for her marriage in light of her husband's job loss. No matter what, she vowed to make their marriage a priority so it would thrive.

She found things that bring her joy. She listens to music while cooking dinner and dances in the kitchen. She journals on the weekends and takes walks with friends by the lake. She listens to comedians on her phone for an uplift while grocery shopping. With the challenges she faces, she has been resolute in finding ways to lighten up and find joy in unexpected places.

So, what is a vow, and what does it have to do with joy?

A vow is a commitment from our values. It guides our actions, especially when we just don't feel like it and particularly when we are in the dark on something. We make vows every day. Some vows go deep and provide unshakable clarity, giving us decisive action. Others ward off problems or difficulties, a shutting down of sorts, as in, "I vow never to tolerate that again."

> *Vows are at the heart of joy!*

Consciously or not, vows are frequent and decisive, and they determine what we do or don't do. They also are the underbelly of true joy.

When we fine tune the use of the vow, massive shifts occur that are powerful. Nothing can stop the power of that vow. No circumstance, no drama, no fear, no possible negative outcome. Frankly, final outcomes don't matter to vows that are that deeply held.

Take Mahatma Gandhi or Mother Theresa. Enough said.

I felt the power of a vow when my late husband was diagnosed with brain cancer. There was a pivotal moment when I didn't know how I could truly keep my heart open with him, knowing he was dying. Then I happened to find my wedding vows. As his sadness grew and his cancer worsened, I read him those vows. Right then, we found hope inside them and found our way to stay connected and loving with each other. I clearly saw that my vow to our marriage had little to do with him. It was my commitment to a sacred agreement, put into words that I spoke to him.

During a very hard session of chemotherapy, David looked at me and tried to say something but couldn't. The cancer had robbed his speech. However, I could read him like a book. He was completely demoralized and questioned why I would continue to love him so much when there was now little for me to receive from him. As I read the vows to him again, I said, "I don't know what you're doing here. But *this*, this vow? That's what I am doing here. So, don't you dare leave me before it's your time." And he didn't. Death is what parted us, and until then, we found joy every day in some way. The vow gave us that.

So, it's important to realize, front and center, the power of a vow. Vows engender determination. They call on a higher power. They allow us to plug into immeasurable joy. Harness vows, and there will be times when you won't recognize yourself or your life. With vows guiding, we can have heart-opening joy and get glimpses into the remarkable human beings that we are.

Plotting Your Course to Joy

- Contrary to the childhood adage about sticks and stones, words can and do hurt. Words are incredibly powerful.

- Words are affirmations that can build a strong country or tear down anything. Treat them like gold because they have a potency beyond what we imagine.
- Consider your own self-talk — the chatter that goes on in your head. Is it positive or negative? One will inspire joy and the other will force joy back into the shadows.
- Create your own personal mantra and practice repeating it until it defines your approach to joy.
- Use affirmations daily in your life to declare your intention for joy.
- Vows are as powerful as words, and the first vow should be to yourself to be open to and embrace joy!

Listen to what Maryl has to say about navigating joy at:
gpstojoybook.com

Chapter Eleven:

Where Is Your Joy G.P.S. Telling You to Go Next?

I realize it might be easy to have *moments* of joy. But what about maintaining and sustaining it? We've talked about the coordinates of joy and how to navigate with them using the Joy Activation Process when new transitions come up or you find challenges you want to shift.

Let's explore various approaches to maintain joy over time. Remember, your mindset gives you the level of joy you experience. There are various ways to stay focused on joy.

Practices to Maintain Joy

So, let's take a look. You'll know what practices will work best for you.

Creativity: Spark your joy with whatever stirs your soul, like music, art, sewing, acting, gardening, etc. My heart-opener is dancing.

Self-care: This seems like the first thing to go! We are so used to putting everything else first before our own bodies! But ignoring our bodies keeps joy in the shadows. Honestly, my friends, where do you drop the self-care ball? Are you actually sleep-deprived, not eating to optimize your body, and ignoring your health-care checkups? Look and see. Are you a hot mess emotionally from being overtaxed? Do you always wear your hair in a ponytail because you don't want to spend the money on great hair care products?

I've learned the hard way. How I treat myself often mirrors my willingness to have joy. How can you up-level here?

Movement: I dance, do yoga, take walks on the beach, and train for strength—all to keep the flow of joy active in my body. As we strengthen our bodies, we expand ourselves for joy. I invite you, from my heart, to move with joy. If you can let it be play, all the better!

Compulsion clarity: Get as clear as you can about your fears and anxieties because they are making decisions for you! Where you experience conflict, angst, or the opposite of what you want, look for clues about issues over which you are suffering. As you uncover them, drop them into the Joy Activation Process to give yourself freedom.

Your non-negotiables: Have you thought about boundaries that need redefining because it's just that time in your life? I occasionally find myself in situations that call for me to make a boundary update. That can be for myself—like, "I'm done *not* fitting in those jeans"—or with others as in, "Please put the dishes in the dishwasher or use the paper plates. The ants are not welcome members of the family!" My non-negotiables evolve as I evolve. It's life.

Write: Words are so powerful. They move things and cleanse. Words make room in our thinking. They are a vehicle to process, connect, contribute, communicate, express, lament, imagine, and uplift. Write your story, write of your love or pain or dreams or joys. You might be surprised that your truths find their way to the surface through your pen!

Mantra: Put your mantra to work. Read it, repeat it to yourself, breathe into it, or share it. Daily repetition lets it flow into your psyche.

Space for the new to emerge: I listen to the ocean outside my bedroom window and the singing birds in my garden. I breathe deeply, all the way to my toes. I meditate and pray words of gratitude. I practice yoga, forgiveness, and much more. Find your way to make space daily where you can.

Connect to love everywhere: with yourself, with your source, with your community. Both internally and outside in your world. One mirrors the other. There is no right place to start. Connect right where you are.

Dancing as Life

Dancing fills me. I am embarrassingly exhilarated whenever I dance. Much to my daughter's chagrin, I miss no opportunity to dance. I dance in the kitchen. I dance my way to the ocean in the morning with earbuds happily plugged into my ears. I dance while I wait in line for my morning hot chocolate. I dance with music I've never heard with steps I've never taken. Dance always brings me joy, and I am now always willing to make it up as I go, no matter how dorky I feel.

I spent several months preparing for a dance competition, and here's what I learned:

1. Dancing shows me how to make peace and move with life's rhythms, letting go of my drive to fight for control, even of the music.
2. As in dancing, life has its own pace, its own rhythm and its own count. Sometimes I select the music, but often I am left with dancing to songs that I didn't choose.

3. When I first hear the music, it seems outside me. When I quiet myself and listen, the music begins to move through me and guide my motion. Once I've danced for a few moments, we unite; I am in harmony with the music and that gives way to my creative expression.

4. To move well, I need to take one step at a time.

5. I can't always follow the music's pace. There are times when I simply lose the rhythm. Then I breathe to center myself and find the flow again.

6. Dancing is my soul's practice. I do it one action at time, one step at time, one mindset at a time.

7. Even when I can't control the elements of the dance experience, I have total control over my attitude, my courage, and my performance.

8. Dancing has helped me grow my ability to adapt and evolve in my own way and time.

9. Competing as a dancer was a dream. Fulfilling that dream enabled me to activate my joy, making a dream come true.

Final Thoughts

Activating your joy is not a destination. It's a path. The compass we use is our mindset, and it gives us a context from which to start.

I believe that we can experience ourselves from our visions and dreams now. Very little can stop fulfilling on those except our self-imposed limits. I've learned that embracing growth is its own process and that as I expand my thinking and heart space, love and joy become palpable, like the beating of my heart.

Joy is not something elusive that needs to be chased. Joy is present and simply needs awareness. Are you ready to activate your joy? Because that answer lies in your hands and heart.

Is there an affirmation you want to claim for yourself that will launch your adventure and create your *G.P.S. to Joy*?

Please put the Joy Scale to work! Let it help you plot where you stand with joy in the different realms of your life. Honest self-reflection will benefit you in spades! Reflect back on the power of your words. Come up with a positively disruptive mantra. (Feel free to review the suggested mantras in the previous chapter.)

Where do you want an up-level? What realm? Which challenge? Grab a cup of joe, take a little time to reflect, and you'll get your answer. You'll need this information to run it through the Joy Activation Process.

You'll find the Joy Activation Process in the following Resource section. Use it, find a friend and navigate your joy together! You'll find others are as ready for joy as you are. I am excited we could come together at this juncture as you embark on using your G.P.S to Joy to get your new bearings and journey in find your new direction!

I look forward to personally connecting with you as your course correction coach and transitions mentor.

In joy,

Maryl Petreccia, #joyexpert
www.activateyourjoy.com
@activateyourjoy
maryl@activateyourjoy.com

For the latest blogs, programs, gifts and new developments, come by and definitely say hello at www.activateyourjoy.com. Nothing adds joy to my own life as much as my ability to help others course correct so that they can navigate their own joy. To pursue this relationship of working together, simply reach out.

Additionally, I invite you to invite me to participate in your book club (remotely or locally in the San Diego area) or to speak on the topic of navigating joy.

Book Club Questions:

1. After reading *GPS to Joy*, what do you see as your biggest challenge or life transition so far?

2. What is one thing that you really want for yourself today?

3. What is one aspect of navigating your transition that you discovered could help you move forward in a positive direction?

4. What is one practice that you use now that ignites joy for you?

5. If you picked one coordinate or "north star" to guide your life by now, what would it be?

6. When transitions happen, do they affect your "joy" condition more or less than before?

7. When you are dealing with a transition, what (if any) practice grounds and centers you?

8. Do you depend on your community to buoy you? If so, what community and what does that entail for you?

9. How do you find that mindfulness, being present, and expressing gratitude give you more capacity to navigate those tough moments?

10. Have these transitions given you a deeper connection to what authentically brings you joy?

11. Did the book and the Joy Activation Process contribute to you? How?

12. What did you like best about this book?

13. What did you like least about this book?

Resources:

Connect with Maryl:

> Website: www.activateyourjoy.com
> Twitter: @activateyourjoy
> Email: maryl@activateyourjoy.com

Helpful Financial Resources:

> www.frugalfanatic.com/budgeting-for-beginners/
> www.frugalfanatic.com/2018-budget-binder/
> Search for books by Suze Orman and Dave Ramsey

Learn Anything:

> www.udemy.com/
> www.coursera.org/

The Joy Activation Process:

Awaken ~ Acknowledge ~ Act ~ Adapt/Allow ~ Affirm
Consciously upgrading and shifting, one issue at a time

Describe the life issue that is challenging you:

_____

Step 1: Awaken
* What SPECIFICALLY do you want instead? What would be a better outcome for you?

_____

_____

Why shift it?

_____

_____

Step 2: Acknowledge
What's the impact on your life from the challenge as it is now? Are you suffering about it?

_____

_____

Step 3: Act – NOW Actions vs NEW Actions
NOW: What actions are you taking now?
1.

2.

3.

NEW: What NEW actions could you take now to achieve your preferred outcome?

NOW Action	Keep/Replace?	NEW Action

Step 4: Adapt

Anchor new actions and allow them to take hold by giving them 3-4 weeks' time to impact your challenge. Write your specific new action(s) and the timeframe you are giving yourself to adapt with the new actions. :

1.

2.

3.

Step 5: Affirm – Yourself and the NEW actions

Check in and see how your new actions are working on that challenge?

Always affirm yourself for being in action! I'll do this in many ways, including creating an affirmation reminder to self that I refer to regularly. I pick one that I feel in my gut.

Here's one I like.

"I take conscious actions to address challenges in my life and I am willing to learn and grow through the transitions I face."

_____

_____

_____

Put the Joy Activation Process to work in your life today!

If you'd like more support with the process, go to www.activateyourjoy.com to connect with me.

Acknowledgments

GPS to Joy began as a love letter to my daughter and my way to fulfill a promise I made to myself and my late husband before he died. I promised that I would continue his legacy to bring joy and healing and that I would make the legacy my own. I deeply wanted to honor our time together and set out to reinvent my life as a daily expression of love, joy, and generosity while I was in the thick of some of the toughest transitions I had ever faced.

My first witness to that promise is my daughter, Helena. Because of her, I dig deep to find courage to go where I've never gone, feel emotions I've never felt, and grow in directions I've never imagined. Her presence has me true myself to what a fulfilled life is now.

Many people have brought this book and my work as a joy coach to life:

Jackie, Lily and Stefan Karnavas, you nourished me for many moons as I got my new bearings.

If I were a table, these stewards of kindness would be the legs holding the top up:

1. The angels at St. Jude Hospital.
2. Annette Gilbert, Connie S., and so many more at Landmark Worldwide.
3. Friends, family, and various people who empower me along the way.

On the writing front, I am deeply grateful for:

Business coach, Marianne Emma Jeff, who spent many hours extracting the foundation for this book. She brought form and words to what started out as tears. Marianne and women at WBMC have been the midwife to birth *GPS to Joy*. Business Coach, Jim Palmer and editor, Ann Deiterich. Editors Mary Ann Tate and Eva Schiess. Their faith in this process continues to call me and *GPS to Joy* forward.

Marcus Bell and Shelita Burke, your faith in me as a messenger for joy cannot be understated.

In closing, I appreciate the outrageously disruptive transitions of my life. Without them, I could not possibly know who I really am and discover life's miracles and gifts. I could not know my depth and dimension. And I could not recognize and celebrate all of this in others. The transitions call me to step into joy, expansion, and to contribute with a new purpose. I truly find joy in helping you activate yours.

In joy,

Maryl Petreccia

About the Author

Maryl Petreccia is known as the #JoyExpert and is the creator of the Joy Activation Process™ – a process born of her own experiences with several highly disruptive and challenging life transitions, including grief.

Having been a successful entrepreneur for over 25 years and after enduring much loss in a short period of time, she learned how to stop suffering and take time to nurture her health, heart, mind, body, soul and her businesses to rediscover and navigate her way back to joy. It was a promise she'd made to her husband before he died. Maryl went from being lost and adrift without a home base to examining each realm of life, then got to work.

A year after his death, at restaurant with a friend, Maryl finally felt immense joy, and her playfulness was unleashed. In that moment, she states, *"I noticed that I didn't have a gaping hole in my heart anymore. I was present and having fun, my guard was down; I felt strong, like I had passed the fragile stage. I realized right then that I had stopped looking for a replacement. I no longer had rooted ties for my identity to anyone nor did I need to be defined by my roles anymore. I felt aligned and connected to me again, finally rooted inside."*

Since business had always been a creative outlet, Maryl decided it was time to create a business from her heart rather than her head. She unfurled her gift for helping people move beyond their transitions and challenges, helping them refuel their joy tanks and plot new paths.

As others began seeking her counsel and coaching, Maryl created the Joy Activation Process™, reverse engineering her own path from surviving losses and life-altering transitions to truly thriving. Today, those facing myriad and often turbulent life transitions (divorce, widowhood, entrepreneurship, empty-nest syndrome, retirement, aging, etc.) have used Maryl's coaching guidance and technique to chart new paths toward new, uplifting relationships, financial growth, progress over stagnation, peace, new opportunities... from being aligned with joy!

Today, Maryl's dreams, wants, and desires have been realized by consciously navigating her joy.

On the home front, she has a home she loves in the rolling hills of North San Diego that buzzes with connection and weekly neighborhood events.

On the friends and community connection front, she has built strong ties in her volunteer work, her business collaborations, her spiritual home, in her local and virtual neighborhoods.

On the romance front, she has found a new normal for love where she gets a daily diet of hugs, kindness, and kisses!

On the well-being and health front, she has daily practices of healthy eating, training, dancing, laughing, meditating, and using words to create worlds through books, blogging, poetry, and more.

On the business front, she is set. Her side gig is being an investor and a boutique owner with friends.

On the coaching and mentoring front, she supports men and women, many of whom have just gone through a major transition (divorce, widowhood, empty nesting, career changes, recalibrating relationships, etc.) to plot out new direction from joy.

And... she has ladies' nights with friends, regularly crashing her new neighbors for dinner in her PJ bottoms... they are regularly amused!